BUNSHA

IMPROVING YOUR BUSINESS THROUGH COMPANY DIVISION

KUNIYASU SAKAI & HIROSHI SEKIYAMA
As Told To David Russell

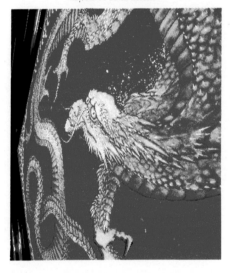

Intercultural Group

New York & Tokyo

Published in the United States by Intercultural Group, Inc.
Edited by Kenichi Miyashita
Cover Design by Kuniharu Suzuki
Front Cover Photo of a tattoo by Hikaru Sasaki
Published in Japan by Taiyo Industry Co., Ltd.
Kisshokai No.2 Kotobuki Bldg, 6-12-1, Ginza, Chuo-ku, Tokyo 104 Japan

Sakai, Kuniyasu, 1928-
[Bunsha. English]
Bunsha: improving your business through company division
/Kuniyasu, Sakai, Hiroshi Sekiyama. As told to David Russell
p. cm. — (ICG pocketbusiness book)
ISBN 1-881267-03-2
1. Conglomerate corporations—Japan-Management. I. Sekiyama, Hiroshi.
II. Title. III. Title: Company division. IV. Series.
HD2756.2.J3S25713 1992
658'.00952—dc20   92-23662 CIP

Second Printing
Printed and Bound in Japan

CONTENTS

Preface

Forty years have passed since I started my first company. Since then, I have made many experiments in the field of company management and expanded my original firm into dozens of companies. In the process, I like to think that I have attained some degree of expertise in the area of business management. I have been fortunate to have had experiences unavailable to the president of any single company; as my companies have grown I have learned first-hand about fields as far apart as manufacturing, real estate, construction, insurance and retailing, among others. This has given me a somewhat unusual perspective on business and a desire to communicate what I have discovered to anyone who is involved in corporate management or concerned about the ways companies can affect the people who work for them.

The philosophy which I have developed as a result of these efforts is not steeped in some strange Oriental mystique, nor is it the kind of conventional business philosophy common in North America and Europe. Managers who have been practicing it for years tell me that it is simple and effective. The only thing wrong with it is that most of the traditional businesses world is pushing in exactly the opposite direction. Being a naturally stubborn sort, this didn't bother me much, but for other managers to put my ideas into action requires an unusual amount of both common sense and guts.

If in the pages that follow I sound at times more like a missionary with a sermon than the head of one of Japan's top high-technology manufacturing groups, it is because I am indeed fanatical when it comes to the subject of business management. I look at my own country, as well as at North America and Europe, and what do I see? Giant conglomerates reeking of waste and inefficiency, top-heavy with overpaid executives with impressive management degrees, but without the slightest idea of how to lead people in a common enterprise, and literally millions of employees who are looking at the clock instead of enjoying their jobs and producing the best work of which they are capable. This situation is, or at least should be, shocking.

And yet we have all come to take it for granted. We are blind to the gross, suffocating inefficiency of this system because we have grown accustomed to it. Moreover, we willingly overlook it or dismiss it as "unavoidable," preferring to look at the magnificence of the system itself. The simple fact is that we are still like little children, fascinated with anything large and powerful. We show almost unquestioning respect for size and power, especially in the corporate world. This is perhaps even more true right here in Japan, so do not expect our big firms to lead any movement to revitalize industry. Sadly, while Japanese companies have changed the way people think about so many things with our "smaller is better" technology, we have not paid attention to our own lessons. We have succeeded in substituting Toyota-thinking for Cadillac-thinking in the world's marketplaces, but in the process we have turned our companies into oversized, inefficient dinosaurs. But the problem is not ours alone. Every industrial nation suffers from the same degenerative disease. It has already sapped the energies of our work forces and it is slowly but surely strangling our biggest companies.

The irony is that there is absolutely no need for this deterioration. The problem is easily curable, if only we recognize it for what it is and have the courage to correct it. The time has come for our industrial monoliths to stop striving for obesity, to turn around, company by company, and begin to revitalize their businesses throughout the world. Moreover, the time has come for the hundreds of thousands of small and medium-size corporations who are the backbone of world business and industry to change their way of thinking, to give thanks that they are indeed still small and to take advantage of this situation to the fullest extent possible.

The key to my system is the guiding principle that "big things stagnate, small ones grow." In the world of business this seems only too clear to me. So, before any company in my group becomes too big and begins to lose its drive, we divide it. I don't mean into little subsidiaries or semi-autonomous divisions. I mean we split it into two or more completely independent corporations with a full complement of administrative departments and totally independent functions for each company. When those companies grow sufficiently, we divide each of them, like a cell dividing itself in two and then both parts dividing again. In other words, what I am about to discuss in these pages is exactly the opposite of rationalization.

Now this may sound like planned inefficiency or the "giant step backwards" to anyone raised in the modern corporate climate of "combine and simplify," but I assure you it is not. I have developed this system only after considerable experimentation, and with every passing year the simple truth of its superiority becomes more and more apparent to me. I only wish I'd realized it forty years ago.

I call this concept *bunsha*, which comes from the Japanese characters for "divide" and "company." I am convinced that—when properly applied—it holds the key to long-term success for any company, in any kind of business, regardless of size or nationality. More than that, it will provide real, lasting satisfaction for both managers and employees. If there is a higher goal in business than healthy growth for companies and individuals alike, I have yet to find it.

Kuniyasu Sakai
Tokyo, January 1989

Note

Throughout this book I often use the word "manager" to refer to every leader in a corporation, from a section chief to a company president. This may seem odd at first—both Japanese and Western corporations are divided into a hierarchy of managers and executives of various levels—but I feel that it makes more sense to emphasize their similar duties to manage and to lead a group of employees than their relative positions in an organizational pyramid. I have grown accustomed to thinking of myself and the many presidents of our group companies as "managers" rather than by titles such as chairman, chief executive officer, managing director, and so forth. Occasionally, when I am speaking specifically about characteristics I think apply to the president of a company, I will use that title to make my meaning clear, but in other cases the term "manager" refers to all leaders, from section chiefs up to and including the president.

Acknowledgments

First of all, although I am always referring to decisions "I" made or ideas "I" had, the truth is that almost everything I have done since I was a teenager has benefited from the sound advice and tireless support of my best friend (and later brother-in-law), Hiroshi Sekiyama. Since our early days he has been content to let me do the talking about our business while he just keeps on working and making things better. I am more indebted to him that I can say. Even though it is my name that appears on the cover, I ask the reader to remember that this book, like our group's success over the past several years, is just as much a product of his efforts as of mine.

I would also like to thank David W. Russell at Tokyo Associates Ltd. for his help in preparing the English manuscript and Kenichi Miyashita at Integrace Japan for handling the innumerable details in bringing this project to fruition.

MY BEGINNINGS
AS A BUSINESSMAN

For several centuries my family has been involved with machinery. After hundreds of years working as blacksmiths, they became machinists in the mid-19th century. When Japan was opened to the outside world in 1867 and new industries sprang up, they became inventors and manufacturers. My grandfather invented an automatic cutting machine which was used by the national tobacco corporation for over 80 years without modification—one of the first steps towards industrial automation in Japan. My father, carrying on this tradition, founded a company which produced precision machinery, and he built up quite a respectable business in the 1920s and '30s. It was into such a family that I was born in 1928, clearly destined to become a machinist of some kind.

While I was still in high school, though, the Tokyo air raids reduced my father's factory to ashes, and we were grateful just to escape with our lives. As the second post-war winter set in, my father took me aside and said, "Kuniyasu, I've been working all my days so that our family could enjoy life when I retire, but the war has taken away everything I had. I am too old to change and too old to start anew. From now on you must become the main support for our family. I will help you in any way I can, but the responsibility is yours." I was so shocked to hear this from my proud, independent father that I didn't know what to say. If such a strong and resourceful man as he could not salvage his buiness from the ashes of Tokyo, how was I going to take over as the head of our household?

Indeed, the war had destroyed almost everything of value in the city. It is hard for those who have not lived through such a time to understand it, and surely harder from our present world of prosperity and comfort to look back on war-stricken Tokyo and try to imagine the feelings of those who lived then. I was seventeen when the war ended and, like many Japanese teenagers, filled with dreams. Despite the devastation all around us, it was for us a time of hope for a brighter future. Perhaps it had to be.

One thing was certain: I had inherited my family's independent spirit. And so, faced with my father's pronouncement that it was time for me to become a man and take care of our family, I decided not to look for work with one of the few firms still operating after the war, but rather, to start my own business.

I learned that the Tokyo Metropolitan School of Industrial Arts from which my father had graduated was still operating, so I enrolled in a six-month course in industrial painting. There I learned the basics of my first trade: painting, coating and enameling various kinds of equipment. At the same time I began scraping together about $500, a used furnace, a spray gun and a fan. Determined that the future would be brighter than the past, I named my new painting company after the Japanese word for "sun." On August 15, 1947, the Taiyo Painting Company was born. I persuaded my best friend, Hiroshi Sekiyama, to join me in this venture, and in no time at all we were ready to conquer the unsuspecting business world. Despite my earlier shock at learning that I was going to be the major support for our family, I now had little doubt that my company would grow and prosper, and I was completely confident about my abilities as a chief executive, for after all, I was already nineteen years old.

Hiroshi and I attacked our work with the passion of youth. We worked day after day, covered with paint, often staying up all night to finish a job, and going for days without sleep. I must surely sound foolish now, but at the time I was determined to build the number – one industrial – painting company in Japan. My obvious lack of any formal business training did not weaken my self-confidence in the slightest. I was a college freshman when I decided to start the company, but almost immediately I stopped going to classes, and soon dropped out altogether. On the day I left, I announced in all seriousness to my classmates that I would someday become the greatest business manager in Japan. Clearly, lack of ambition was not my greatest problem.

Taiyo got off to a slow start and struggled for several years. We advertised that we would do any kind of painting work, and as a result, we took on a wide variety of jobs, many of which can still move me to either laughter or tears when I remember them now. Hiroshi and I lived with paint permanently decorating our faces and our hair. A photo from those days shows a couple of scrawny, smiling kids in paint-stained T-shirts and dirty pants, which was how we looked for the first few years of our business. We are standing in front of a couple of dilapidated wooden buildings which served as our first "factories." These buildings were permeated with the smell of various paints and chemicals, and our one small fire extinguisher was more a talisman to ward off the unthinkable than any real protection. For many years I would awaken suddenly and sit bolt upright in bed at just the smell of smoke from a neighbor's stove or the sound of a distant siren. I knew very well that all our work could disappear overnight.

Gradually, though, we were able to expand, hire more staff, build metal-walled plants, and install modern safety devices. We purchased more furnaces and focused on real industrial painting, coating products such as bicycle and motorcycle parts, lamps, utensils for the Occupation forces, window frames for a major Japanese car maker, and so on. Little by little, business began to pick up.

Although I had barely begun to learn the craft that was paying our bills, something in the Sakai blood must need to be around machinery, and before long I had decided to expand into metal stamping as well. I invested what little profits we had in more equipment and built facilities for our new business. This delighted my father, who knew nothing about painting, but felt right at home in a machine shop. He helped to maintain the machinery and advised us on every aspect of our new trade. We continued hiring new staff, sometimes finding men with experience in related fields, sometimes taking in young men with no training whatsoever and teaching them the skills they needed right at our factory. Within just four years of Hiroshi's and my shaking hands we had over fifty full-time employees plus several part-time workers from around the neighborhood. In that year I realized that the firm would be not merely a painting concern, and so I renamed it Taiyo Industries Corp. ("Taiyo Kogyo K.K." in Japanese).

The Japanese economy began to recover during the early 1950s, and Taiyo Industries grew with it. Orders came in steadily and the costs of our materials began to decline. We continued to build new factories, expand our old ones, hire new personnel and diversify our business. We had a small fleet of vehicles when most companies had none, and production equipment which at that time other firms could only dream of acquiring. We sometimes had to invent our own equipment to satisfy our clients' demands, but thanks to my father's ingenuity and the tireless efforts of our staff, we were able to fulfill every contract.

As the years went by it became clear that electronic equipment was growing into a major industry, and we branched out yet again to handle an increasing amount of this business. One of our regular customers was a rapidly growing electronics firm much larger than ourselves which I shall refer to herein as "Miyamoto Electronics." We were producing a variety of parts for radios and other electronic equipment for them, and thus, in a sense, sharing in their growth. As fast as we could fill orders for Miyamoto, bigger orders seemed to follow, and so we quickly shifted more and more of our production facilities to meet their needs. Without realizing it, we soon became quite dependent on their business, and this was soon to be the source of our problems for years to come.

But I'm already getting ahead of myself. At the time we are discussing, the late 1950s, the post-war labor movement was in full swing and I found my labor costs rising rapidly. Although I was working harder than ever, and the company was in an excellent position to grow, our profit margins seemed leaner than ever. I worked harder still, but profits kept slipping away. My joy in running my own business began to evaporate.

It was at this time that I first discovered the real meaning of a very obvious principle. Unfortunately, it is one of those abstract ideas to which we pay only lip service unless we experience it first-hand. That is, man works to be rewarded, not only through monetary compensation, but also through the satisfaction of doing his work. If his continuous labor is not compensated in both ways, it is nothing more than slavery of one form or another. And this is just what was happening to me. I was working as hard as I knew how, but not enjoying the fruits of my labors. There seemed no answer in sight. True, the fact is that I was not a good manager or I would have found a solution to my firm's problems much earlier. But I had chosen my own path, and now I had to learn the hard way how to run a company.

I looked around Taiyo Industries and I began to realize that many of our workers had been on the job for almost ten years, and they were growing too routinized. When the company was brand new they shared Hiroshi's and my excitement in building a new firm, but now that we had grown so much, it was only natural that they should lose some of their interest in the job. I understood even then that every business needs to rejuvenate its internal system from time to time, which is one of the basic principles of *bunsha*, although the full implications of that system had not yet dawned on me.

However, I did remember how often my father had said, "If a man can be his own master and work on his own initiative rather than under another's rule, he can always perform better. His responsibilities increase, of course, but so does his sense of controlling his own life. There is no greater motivating force in our world than man's yearning for freedom." I realized that if my company was to survive, I must take advantage of this aspect of human nature to revitalize Taiyo Industries. Why not give each worker a freer hand, I thought. Why not let each one find the best way to do his job, and then reward those who succeed? Rather than trying to cut costs in every possible way, as we had been doing, perhaps we should spend a little more where it would do the most good— in improving each employee's sense of accomplishment.

Thus it happened that in 1958 I set up a system of incentives and asked one of my key managers to refine the system so that it would both emphasize worker independence and reward quality work. At the same time, I decided to hand over a large part of my management responsibilities (which until then I had shared only with Hiroshi) to a group of senior workers. I entrusted everything to them: obtaining orders, delivering products and collecting bills. I organized the firm into sections and made a group of employees into section chiefs, responsible for trading, production, adminstration, etc. Each had the authority to determine pricing, production goals, personnel changes or policies within his section. I think I surprised them by giving them even more autonomy than they had expected. I not only entrusted them with a section of the company's business, but also told them to set their own monthly goals.

To make the purpose and nature of the new system clear to every man in the company, we held a series of briefings which we called "ripple meetings." These were progressively larger meetings at which the same topic was discussed for the benefit of different levels of the staff. First, we held a meeting of our executive managers and explained the new system; then we held another meeting, again with the executive managers in attendance, but this time including the division managers; then another meeting with the executive and division managers, but expanding the group to include middle managers as well; finally, we met with the new section chiefs, who would have to communicate directly with every employee in the company. This meant that the executive managers had to go through the same explanation four times, but it allowed us to revise and polish the system as we progressed through these "ripples." It also allowed those in higher positions to get a better idea of what the system was all about and how those under them were reacting to it. Moreover, every time we held a meeting with a larger group, the managers who had been through it before came to have a greater sense of responsibility, a feeling that they were really in charge of part of the company.

I originally proposed to give every worker a cash bonus for attaining a goal which was mutually agreed upon. Later I decided to give the incentive beforehand rather than to promise it after the goals were attained. I came to realize that profit-sharing is far more effective when done in advance, and so I paid the bonus up front, thinking it would stimulate our employees to work even harder. I took a chance on this "all or nothing" method and the response surprised even me.

Almost overnight the company began to rejuvenate. Within a few days the offices looked fresh and vital; even the appearance of my staff began to change. Individuals, both line workers and managers, took a new interest in the company's profits, and soon they began posting graphs on the walls to show monthly sales records, unit costs and so on. Everyone tackled their work with a fresh attitude and seemed eager to improve on the previous month's results. When the factory workers, many of whom were lacking enthusiasm just a few weeks before, started paying closer attention to their work, the number of inferior products decreased and production speed increased. Our sales staff obtained higher orders and were likewise rewarded with a bonus. Superior quality, teamwork and maximum effort became the norm. When customers visited the factories, our employees proudly showed off their work. I was awestruck.

Perhaps today, thirty years later, this idea may seem a bit simplistic. Profit – sharing plans are common enough these days, although I still think advance incentives are a bit unusual. Still, it was only one step towards revitalizing our company, a small step on the way towards *bunsha*. But for me, in 1958, it was an eye-opener.

Needless to say, our "rebirth" as a company attracted the attention of our customers, and orders began to flow in. Customer satisfaction became a matter of course. Soon both the plant and the individual employees were operating at full capacity, and this energy fueled our rapid expansion over the next few years. Our success also attracted the media, and we were besieged by newspaper and magazine reporters, university professors and government officials. Eventually, as managers all over Japan began to read about the Taiyo system in business journals, a number of them came to visit our plant to see for themselves. I was asked to give lectures around the country on what I simply called my "experiment."

Yet, despite our explosive growth and the spotlight of media attention, I was not satisfied. For one thing, the system could not last indefinitely. Over the years I phased out the cash incentives and put more emphasis on improving the working environment so that our staff could both earn a good wage and enjoy their work. I continued to promote promising young men, making them section and division managers and giving them responsibility for every aspect of the business of their unit. And the company continued to grow.

By the early 1960s we were getting to be a fairly sizable concern. Whereas once I could gather all the managers in my office to hash out a problem, we now had an organizational chart like a giant pyramid. I no longer knew each of our employees personally and I was beginning to grow more distant from the work in the factories. For some time I had taken charge of our sales operations, as I believed this was the key to our future growth. Now, "sales promotion" in Japan means more than just explaining your products' features to prospective clients, offering technical support and the usual kinds of service. An intrinsic part of Japanese business, then as now, is socializing—a polite term for taking clients out to the very best restaurants, geisha houses, hostess bars and so forth, and spending inordinate quantities of both time and money to see that they are happy. I didn't know much about wining and dining in fancy places, but I was quite willing to put the "promotional" resources of the company at the disposal of my clients on a Friday evening, and they were only too willing to show me how to spend them.

Thus, I was increasingly finding myself in Tokyo's fabled Ginza district (which even back then was expensive, I assure you), looking like a typical company president, entertaining current and prospective customers for Taiyo Industries. Although I was not good at flattering people, had no "social presence" and cared little for drinking, I have to admit that I quickly learned to enjoy this easy life. I rationalized it all by telling myself it was a kind of compensation for the years of hard work I had put into starting and building up the company. In this I began to feel a vague discomfort, although I didn't really see it for what it was until somebody put me in my place, and without mincing any words. Who would have the nerve to tell the president of a successful company to get his act together "or else"? Not his stockholders. Not his employees or his customers. No, it was someone with real clout.

One day I received a letter from my

mother. It said in short, "While you're off having fun in fancy restaurants and expensive bars, sleeping late every morning and making 'play' into work, your company is drifting like a ship without a captain. Of course, Hiroshi is back at the factory with his shirt-sleeves rolled up, working all night long, as usual, and trying to hold things together. But you're supposed to be the president. Everyone looks up to you as the leader and they expect you to be there to guide them and run the show when problems arise. You will not let them down. You are a Sakai."

I was shocked and totally disgusted with myself. How could I have so easily fallen into this trap? I had let down both my company and my best friend. In fact, Hiroshi was no longer just my best friend, for a few years before he had married my only sister, and so, while I had always thought of him like a brother, we were now really brothers-in-law. And how was I repaying him for all his support and hard work? How I despised myself that day!

I returned to our factory at once and told Hiroshi that as of that moment he was in charge of sales; I wanted nothing more to do with it, and I felt he more than deserved a reward for "holding the fort" while I had deserted my post. In fact, as it turned out, Hiroshi's natural warmth and humility made him an ideal person to handle sales promotion, and he was soon bringing in new orders at a pace I could never have imagined, so the arrangement worked out well both for us and for Taiyo.

By the mid-'60s Japan was already well into the electronics age, and Taiyo Industries was heavily involved in all sorts of electronic-parts manufacture. We did what is now commonly called "OEM" or Original Equipment Manufacture; in other words, we made electronic parts so that another firm could assemble them and sell the finished products under its own name. In fact, we still do a great deal of OEM work, and many of our companies make both parts and finished products for some of Japan's top electronics firms (which is why you will never see a product with the Taiyo name on it—we are OEM manufacturers). But back then we had only a single major client, whom I referred to earlier by the name Miyamoto Electronics. They were soon to become one of Japan's best-known electronics firms, and their steady flow of orders fueled our own expansion. As I mentioned before, we discovered too late that Taiyo Industries had become increasingly dependent on Miyamoto. Although we were quite content to be a subcontractor, we had come to exist, as do the vast majority of Japanese firms, under the shadow—or perhaps, I should really say, at the mercy—of a much larger company that cared nothing about our survival or internal difficulties so long as we could produce for it.

This in itself might not seem so unusual to my Western readers, but the fact that we were virtual prisoners of this system, bound eternally by a code of loyalty to Miyamoto's corporate group, must seem rather odd to those who are not familiar with the Japanese subcontractor system. In fact, I still feel so strongly about the inequities of this system—which is to this day the backbone of many Japanese industries, not only manufacturing—that I have included a separate section about it at the end of this book. Consequently, I will not go into detail here about Taiyo's bonds to Miyamoto. Suffice to say that having become a supplier in their network, we now found ourselves shackled by chains of obligation and threatened with punishment if we should stray.

Being full of the idealism with which I had started out in business, I resented this state of servitude. Why should my company be forever in bondage to some giant firm? I thought. However, truth to tell, I was also scared, and with good reason: If I did anything to offend Miyamoto Electronics and they were to terminate orders to us, our main source of revenue would disappear, salaries and bank loans would be forfeited and I would lose the company. Taiyo would not be the first firm to go under in such a fashion. The subcontractor knows he is valued only so long as he does what he is told and does not complain.

On the other hand, Miyamoto had already found a number of occasions—for purely economic reasons—to halt their orders to us. From time to time we experienced long periods of severe cutbacks with no recourse but to wait for the renewed generosity of our "master." Needless to say, we were not allowed to have any business dealings with other firms. In spite of my fears, I couldn't help but wonder how much longer we could go on like this, and I began to search for ways to escape.

In 1965, one of my managers suggested that, since our electronics business had now become so important to the company, we should open a separate plant to manufacture condensers and printed circuit boards. I agreed, but I felt that land and construction costs were much too high in Tokyo, and with the unreliability of Miyamoto's orders, I thought it best to economize by building this factory somewhere outside the city. I proceeded to rent a suitable site in Tochigi Prefecture, just northeast of the capital, and moved our condenser and PC board divisions to Taiyo's new detached factory.

In 1967 another big firm approached Taiyo and asked if we could produce PC boards on short notice. Our machines and our crew had been idle for several weeks, and I finally felt I had no other choice. I accepted the order without informing Miyamoto. But before long our regular orders began to come in again, and as they increased we were forced to stop producing for our new client. They were furious, of course—they had been counting on our production to meet their own orders—and so our return to the "master's house" meant the end of our business relations with a new and potentially very good client. I'm sure this must seem insanity from the point of view of Western business, but in Japan it is totally unthinkable to turn one's back on the firm which has been your "benefactor." We must remain eternally indebted to that firm, even if it has not always treated us well in the past.

Clearly, the small subcontractor's situation is an endless cycle of reward and suffering, but never because of his own efforts, and it is this that tore at my insides. Yet, I would not be disloyal. Our only hope, I told our managers, was to stand out among the many subcontractors in our field, and thus earn a favored position in Miyamoto's hierarchy. As I expected, our men redoubled their efforts, and the company performed with an efficiency that made me proud. Each section worked as if it were an independent firm, and each section chief learned for himself the secrets of good management, offering guidance and encouragement to his subordinates, working with them rather than browbeating them. As a result, we attained our target: we delivered top-quality products faster than any other plant in the Miyamoto Group.

Although it had many small companies to choose from, Miyamoto began to give more and more of its orders to Taiyo. Thanks to our efficiency and constant emphasis on quality control, we soon found ourselves flooded with orders. Although still a "slave" company, at least our talents were being appreciated, I thought, and perhaps the future would be a little brighter.

Then one day one of the managers at Miyamoto said that it was unfair to give all the company's orders only to Taiyo Industries, and that our orders should be reduced and redistributed for the benefit of competing subcontractors. I was stunned. The manager who made this suggestion probably did so at the request of several of the other subcontractors, and I could appreciate their position. But this was a matter of vital importance to a small plant like ours. We had been producing to our utmost potential, and what were we to receive for our efforts? More cutbacks?

I decided to go in person to the magnificent corporate headquarters of Miyamoto Electronics and speak to their president. Of course I did not need to profess our loyalty to his firm, as this is taken for granted in Japan. Rather, I told him with sincerity and great pride that my firm was working to its fullest potential, and that I and every single member of my staff would spare no energy in helping Miyamoto to grow by achieving any targets they set for us.

The president was brief but to the point. "I thank you for your devotion, Mr. Sakai," he said, "but your words are like an expression of deep compassion from an ugly woman."

Looking back now, I can better understand his reaction. But at that time I was so young, perhaps thirty-seven or -eight, and I felt he had cruelly insulted not only me but every member of my firm. I was furious. By the time I returned to my office I was determined to find some way out of this predicament, even if it broke my company in two. And as a matter of fact, that's just what it did.

Although I feared for the future of Taiyo, I also saw no merit in maintaining the relationship with Miyamoto Electronics as it was. After surveying the market, I concluded that the demand for PC boards was likely to increase in the near future, and so, under these conditions, it was a favorable time to make a radical change. My only option was to establish a new company, producing for any customer who wanted quality merchandise. Thus, in September 1968, I decided to turn our Tochigi factory into a legally separate entity, and Daisho Denshi K.K. was born. To get it started properly, I invested funds from Taiyo Industries that were badly needed for our own development. I also asked Hiroshi to take the reins as president of the new company.

When Miyamoto Electronics heard of it, they thought it was a declaration of open revolt. In fact, rebellion was not my motive; by this point I had no specific quarrel with Miyamoto; my single aim was to have a company that I could operate freely and to be able to sell to whomever I chose, including Miyamoto. After considerable thought, I decided I must find a way to pacify them. Perhaps you begin to see the depth to which the concept of belonging to an industrial "group" permeates the thinking of the Japanese subcontractor. Where any Western manager would have long since given up trying, I still believed that it was essential to maintain some kind of relations with Miyamoto by any means possible. I went to their offices and told them that a violent quarrel had arisen between myself and Hiroshi. I said that Hiroshi had left Taiyo vowing to establish his own firm, and that this was the origin of Daisho Denshi. A pretty thin ruse, I admit, but I was desperate.

Of course, as I have explained, Hiroshi and I have been close friends since we were children, and business partners since I founded Taiyo. The people at Miyamoto must have known this, and also that we were brothers-in-law; and yet, I prayed that this simple trick would allow Taiyo Industries to take the brunt of Miyamoto's wrath and at the same time give Hiroshi's firm an opportunity to start afresh as a completely independent contractor.

Unfortunately, we never got to see how well the plan might have worked, for no sooner was Daisho Denshi established than it crossed swords with Miyamoto on a very important project. Our new firm was eager to grow, and very quickly entered into an agreement to buy a patented production theory from a certain American company. It turned out that Miyamoto also wanted to bid on the same patent. Of course, when they heard that Taiyo was negotiating with the U.S. firm, Miyamoto wired them not to sell us the patent rights, but it was too late.

(Just as an aside, it might be interesting to note that several large Japanese companies, including some very famous firms, also purchased those patent rights. However, in the end Daisho Denshi beat all of them in successfully applying the theory. Although the other companies possessed both high levels of technology and enormous capital, they were too quick to give up their R&D efforts, while we made experiments day and night, determined to implement the theory. Finally, after many sleepless nights and frustrated days, we developed the know-how to put the theory to work, and it has since served us to great advantage. To this day we continue to pay the American firm a patent fee of several million dollars annually. Perhaps, I began to think, the operations of smaller companies can actually be more effective than those of their big rivals. Why is it we succeeded where they failed? I now question how hard the employees of some of these huge companies attacked the problem and how seriously their managers urged them on.)

Hiroshi was soon summoned to Miyamoto Electronics, where one of the executives said to him, "We won't give you any trouble on one condition: you do business only with us. Is that clear?" This is typical of the way large firms deal with their subcontractors, and we were more or less expecting it, but all the same, Hiroshi was crushed. To yield to this threat would mean all our efforts were in vain, but to stand against a company as powerful as Miyamoto could mean the end of both our firms.

Although Daisho Denshi was born of my own company, I had already promised Hiroshi and his staff total independence, even from me. Thus, I went only as an outside advisor to meet with the executives at Daisho. I begged them to refuse Miyamoto's demands. "Don't knuckle under to this pressure or we're right back where we started," I said, "If we survive this, we can do business with anyone; we're free! And if we don't, I'd rather start again with nothing than watch both our companies knuckle under to those guys. Let's fight it out." My words were brave, but I knew there was no reason for their managers to see things my way. Their company was now truly independent of mine and, pro-

MY BEGINNINGS AS A BUSINESSMAN

viding it went along with Miyamoto's demands, it had a bright future. I knew that Hiroshi would stand by me no matter what, as I would for him, but now he had a responsibility to his own company and to his employees. Why shouldn't they work for Miyamoto and, like hundreds of other firms, make the best profits they could and be a success?

I made it clear to him that I understood the situation and did not expect him to influence his managers. But what I had not counted on was what their earlier experience at Taiyo Iudustries had meant to these men, and to my surprise even the lower-ranking managers voted that we should stand together. Looking back on it, perhaps that was the day our group was born, the first time we realized that we could exist independently as companies, even compete with each other when necessary, but pull together and help each other in times of trouble. I was proud and elated. But I knew the battle was yet to start, and I had no doubt about where the attack would come from.

Before long, a high-ranking executive from Miyamoto came to call at my office. His voice was cool and threatening. "Mr. Sakai, your attitude is most uncooperative. Do I need to spell out what will happen if you don't stop this foolishness immediately? First, we'll cut off all business with the Taiyo firms, and then pass the word around to make sure no one else will touch you. Where will you be? You'll be lucky to get a job helping some old geezer run a radio repair shop in Hokkaido." I waited a long time before replying, and when I did he knew I meant business: "You forget that I am one of your stockholders. If you try to cut us off, I will show up at your next shareholders' meeting and cause such a scene, you'll wish you'd never heard of me or my company. I will publicly demand the resignation of your president on grounds of incompetence. I will take full advantage of the media coverage of the ensuing scandal, and use every possible means I can find to expose you. Unless you kill me, I guarantee I won't stop until I see a public boycott of all Miyamoto products." In Japan, where even saying such things, much less doing any of them, is totally unthinkable, the shock on my visitor's face said I had hit home, and the tone of my voice was enough to send him packing.

Our orders from Miyamoto resumed, as I'd thought they would, but relations went into a predictable decline. Around that time I also began to discover some of the problems that can arise when company division is not well thought out. In the early days some of our staff knew almost nothing about producing PC boards. I had started the new company with a mixture of experienced and inexperienced work ers and a few men whom our section chiefs had labeled "expendable," meaning they were not especially productive and didn't seem to care about their work. This was a grave mistake in judgment that I never made again, but even so, it taught me a lesson about what a good manager and a new environment can do for unmotivated workers.

One of the managers at Daisho was a man of boundless energy. His confidence and his drive fired up that crew and turned the unskilled, unenthusiastic laborers into a first-rate manufacturing operation in record time. Most interesting to me was how the new working environment completely transformed those whom other managers had given up on as "dead-wood." Tossed unexpectedly into a stormy sea, they kicked and struggled and soon learned to swim, proving to me that they weren't "bad" workers at all, only that for some reason they hadn't been adequately motivated in their old jobs. In its first year the new firm's total sales were a miserable $26,000. Fifteen years later they topped $87 million. Yes, indeed, strange things seemed to happen when I started up new companies, even if some of the employees were less than ideally motivated to begin with. It was at this point that I began to see how dividing a company can create a challenging atmosphere that brings out the best in people—people who might otherwise be content simply to put in their time and do mediocre work.

In addition to the tremendous efforts by all its employees, another factor that accounted for the new firm's success was the support it received from its "parent". Taiyo Industries continued to back the new company financially until it grew strong. A newly divided company, like a newborn baby, must be nurtured or it will not survive. In Japan we say, "All's well that starts well." I financed the company because I believed in it, and I knew that despite the limitations it had been forced to accept, it would perform satisfactorily if given a chance. Since that time this has become part of our philosophy in setting up new corporations: give them good leaders (and let the leaders choose their own staff), solid financial support and plenty of time to stand on their own feet.

I still remember the day I officially broke with Miyamoto Electronics. It was on July 3, 1970, that I told them openly that I was still willing to accept their orders, but that from then on Taiyo Industries was completely independent and would work for any company that requested its services. They considered my announcement for some time. Their reply reflects perhaps better than anything I could say the position which Japan's giant corporations even today maintain vis-à-vis their many subcontractors: Miyamoto would allow me to accept outside orders, they said, but only if Taiyo paid Miyamoto a certain percentage of its sales every year as a kind of "commission." Needless to say, I told them what they could do with this proposal. They were enraged.

By this point, however, I did not much care. We now had three companies involved in the still-growing electronics field, and the newest of them was even filling orders for Miyamoto, while the other two developed new business at a rapid pace. Now that I was truly independent and business was on the right track, I had a bit of time to reflect upon my successes and failures.

The more I looked at our companies' growth and problems over the years, the more I saw the need to keep a firm at a manageable size and then to manage it directly and openly, not from afar or through some labyrinthine chain of command. I spent some time walking through our factories and was genuinely proud of the work I saw there. Employees at all levels were finding satisfaction in their work. Absenteeism, illness, poor productivity, careless mistakes and the like had all but disappeared from all three companies.

It could not be pure chance, I told myself. Somehow, through trial and error, some common sense and a bit of luck we had developed a system of running a company in which everyone benefited. The results were obvious. At one of our factories a couple of workers had started a union, but membership never grew and finally it was disbanded (the problem was apparently that my goals for improving working conditions were more radical then the union's). Not only were our employees happy, but our clients were delighted. We were producing high-quality components at very reasonable prices with a negligible return rate.

Throughout the ordeal with Miyamoto Electronics I had thought, "They can push us around because we're small. When Taiyo gets big enough, this will never happen again." I suppose the president of every small and medium-size company dreams of his firm growing severalfold and becoming a force to be reckoned with in the marketplace. I, too, had had such dreams. But I finally came to realize that many of Miyamoto's problems were actually rooted in its too-rapid growth. It had become too big and too powerful, and its executives too isolated from realities outside their boardroom. In short, the firm was no longer manageable. I vowed that, one way or another, this would never happen to our firms.

And then I looked at our "group" objectively. True, they were relatively small companies compared with giants like Miyamoto, but they were three healthy companies, growing steadily, with hardworking, committed managers and dedicated staff. We knew where every penny came from in each company and where it went, what our costs were for every section for every week for every item. Nothing was "missing," "not yet inventoried," or "to be accounted for." Each firm was trim, well run and a good place to work. At last it began to dawn on me that there was only one thing that could destroy all this—our own growth. If any of our firms were to grow too big, it would lose the vital edge that made it both a tough competitor and an interesting place to work. Indeed, I began to see that the biggest enemy of any healthy, well-managed company is not its competition but itself. In striving for growth, which is every company's rightful goal, many fall into the trap of uncontrolled growth, which is ultimately destructive.

I began to fine-tune my ideas through constant discussions with Hiroshi and the other managers of our three firms. We determined from that day forward to make Taiyo not merely a prosperous group of companies, but a strong, dynamic and constantly expanding enterprise—one that would never succumb to the problems of corporate obesity. This was the true beginning of *bunsha*.

As our firms continued to grow over the next few years, we established half a dozen new companies. And those companies in turn gave birth to others, and so on. Today each one is still healthy and growing; each contributes in some way to the strength of the group, as each was supported in its early years by the strength of the group. Although I am no longer officially connected with the management of any of these firms, they are all in a way like my own children, and I am very satisfied with their performance. The total number of firms is large, but each company remains relatively small. Each one is complete and independent in itself. Each has its own operation and exists and prospers on its own merits. They do not share a common group name with which to "reassure" clients that they are actually much bigger than they appear; rather, each has an independent name to affirm its basic independence. While they all belong to the Taiyo Group, it is (unlike other such groups) both cooperative and at the same time competitive. In this respect, their smallness is their strength.

I attribute the group's steadily increasing market share in numerous fields to the fact that each plant within the group handles its business independently, and so retains its competitive spirit. Occasionally two members of the group will find themselves handling the same products, and so they will naturally compete with each other. This is not a common practice in Japanese corporate families, and I am often asked why I permit it. "I don't think there's anything wrong with it," I say. "In fact, I think it's in everyone's best interest. If a firm can stay lean and productive, it will never want for customers. But if any of our firms ever gives up constantly striving to be competitive, it will surely lose its position in the market before long. In that case I would much rather see it sacrifice its market share to another Taiyo Group company and learn a lesson in the process." The group does not exist to subsidize poor performance among its member companies.

Today, as I write this, we have a few dozen companies, and by the time this book is published there may well be another dozen or more. I have no wish simply to watch our number of firms increase; that would be pointless. Instead, our object is to divide companies only when they are ready, and when that time comes, I am delighted to see that our managers have the sense to let their businesses grow in the healthiest way possible: by division.

Just to bring this short history of the Taiyo family to a conclusion, I should mention that in 1978 I resigned as president of Taiyo Industries. I had been at the helm for over thirty years, and that's long enough. One of the prime benefits of *bunsha* is that it provides room for employees to advance much faster than in a normal company structure. Regularly promoting your subordinates is one important way to keep a company young and energetic. So when I reached the age of fifty I decided it was time to let in some new blood. I handed over the reins of Taiyo Industries to another manager and became an advisor to the firm. This allowed me the freedom to set up a small office in Ginza and do what I most wanted to do in life: advise other businessmen on how to deal with their own management problems—in particular, how to improve their companies so as to unlock the tremendous potential energy of their employees. Of course, I still like to meet with Taiyo's managers and talk with employees at all levels. And every one of them knows that I am never "in a meeting" if they need to call, and the door to my office is always open if they should want to visit. Does that sound like a burden for an ex-president? I don't think so. And if you were to drop by my office in Ginza, I bet you'd swear I was the happiest manager in Japan.

COMPANY
DIVISION

Why divide a company at all?

It is no secret that we Japanese love baseball, both the professional games and the nationally televised high school tournaments. It is a rare coffee shop that doesn't have a TV on during the baseball season, and you must occasionally forgive the more energetic among the patrons for cheering out loud when their team makes a great play or scores a run. Even fans of other teams or other sports may find themselves drawn into the excitement at a time like this. Something in us just seems to respond naturally to the sight of a team overcoming their own physical limitations, the challenge of tough competition, and the complexities of the game itself to emerge triumphant. And when you see one of those rare games where a team just comes alive, where every player is "on," where difficult plays suddenly seem routine and the team looks invincible, it's electrifying. The manager is sending signals to his players, each one is adjusting quickly to the other team's movements and every man is playing like it is the most important game of his career. Even the bottom of the line-up is hitting for extra bases, the pitcher has found a form everyone thought he lost years ago, and the fielders are running their hearts out to make impossible diving catches. Before you know it your blood is pumping, your heart is racing and, even though you're sitting in front of a television miles from the ball park, you find yourself instinctively cheering.

Haven't you every seen a "perfect game," be it baseball, football, rugby or whatever, when every player seemed to be giving 100% and the team looked invincible? You probably went home saying, "If they play like that all season, they could hang out the pennant right now." We all seem to respond instinctively to the sight of good athletes working together, performing at their peak potential both individually and as a team, and we are especially thrilled when the game brings out the best in all its players.

Now, just for a moment, let's imagine that the same game was played with three or four times the number of players on a side. Let's go back to baseball for our example. Let's put thirty or so men out in the field at the same time, add a few extra coaches and a half-dozen assistant managers to help control the situation. What happens? Efficient communication between the dugout and the field disappears immediately, routine plays become incredibly complex and the individual performance of each player drops off very quickly. Why run for that fly ball? Let the next guy grab it; after all, he's closer, right? Imagine a whole season played with thirty men on a side. What would happen to the motivation and performance of the individual players?

It almost seems as if there is some natural law about the ideal number of players for various team efforts, doesn't it? Five players on a side makes for a pretty wild and sloppy baseball game, but several times that number makes it far too cumbersome. That doesn't mean you can't play and it doesn't mean you can't win, only that you're wasting a lot of talent and overlooking a lot of inefficiency in the process.

Exactly the same thing holds true for a business. There is an appropriate size for every organization. If a company remains at a manageable size, it is certain to develop. If it grows too fast or too large, it exceeds its appropriate size and efficiency declines. Of course, it can still function, just as a baseball team can play with thirty or forty men on a side. But would you want to buy a ticket?

Why divide a company? The reason is obvious: the smaller the company, the more efficiently it runs. Every manager in every company in the world knows this already in his heart, but we all tend to overlook it in our constant striving to become big.

What good is a stuffed tiger?

In Japan, the "smaller is better" philosophy has proved a valuable guiding principle for our manufacturing industries, re-shaping our thinking about everything from IC circuits to automobiles, but it has yet to be viewed as a goal by the companies that produce these goods. Japanese companies, like their North American and European counterparts, generally aspire to become giant combines, employing thousands of people, amassing billions of dollars in sales and, ultimately, influencing national policies. These firms are listed on stock exchanges and their shares are called "blue chips" to show the respect we have for such pillars of the commercial community.

All this is well and good. I have no quarrel with giant corporations per se. I wish them every success, because many of them are my clients. But I have no desire to be like them, and I certainly do not envy their managers. What manager in his right mind wants to be in charge of thousands of workers he doesn't know, plants he has never visited, products he knows next to nothing about? It is a glutton's dream of power, to rule over a kingdom of the lazy, the inefficient and the unknown. To me this has nothing to do with real business management, and while I will be the first to admit that there are some brilliant executives of such corporate behemoths, I will also be the first to point out that their number is exceedingly small.

In Japan we have a saying: "What good is a stuffed tiger?" A big corporation may look powerful and impressive on the outside, but if in reality it is merely big and soft, it has no meaning. We respect it for the power it once had, but we know that it is no longer lean and hungry. Ultimately, such an institution will fail. Of course, it will not collapse overnight, but sooner or later there will come a time when it cannot respond to changes in the business environment, when its own staff becomes more of a hindrance than an asset. A company must never allow this to happen; it must always be aggressive, always driving forward. It must never get so big that its main job is merely to preserve its own status quo, but always be oriented towards growth. The larger a company becomes, the less its individual workers are capable of contributing to its growth. As a result, they lose interest in their work and feel less and less connected with the firm. As this condition progresses, it affects every part of the company, like a disease spreading throughout the corporate body. Seminars and company trips will not cure it. Extra holidays and bonuses will not cure it. The body will weaken and eventually die.

If a company controls its growth, however, it preserves a healthy condition which stimulates workers naturally and thus motivates productivity. A healthy company is an organization in which each worker can perform to his potential, like an athlete on a well-balanced team.

Good managers aim to make the company just such a team. A mid-sized firm, not too big or too small, is ideal; managers can gauge the mood of each employee at the morning meeting. When a company grows much bigger, the managers gradually lose control of the team and the employees lose sight of their individual assignments and contributions to the organization as a whole.

In dividing a company, the baton is passed to the next generation. Just as a relay team is able to reach a distant goal much faster than a single runner, a "team" of companies will achieve meaningful success in a shorter time and support each other when hard times inevitably come along.

Dividing a company for the wrong reasons

Dividing a large or medium-sized company is nothing new in Japan. It happens all the time. But it happens for the wrong reasons. For one thing, there are substantial tax advantages to splitting a company into a parent firm and several wholly or partly owned subsidiaries. Tax attorneys often advise managers of larger firms to consider dividing their companies to increase tax deductible write-offs and curtail taxable property. But this has nothing to do with what I mean by *bunsha*. A wise executive will divide his company whether there are tax advantages or not. He will divide it even if there are tax disadvantages. This is how strongly I believe in *bunsha*.

In our country, it is easy to establish a company. Anyone can do it. The owner of a little pushcart food stand can become a "president," and his wife can become a "managing director." If the couple goes somewhere for a holiday, they can report the whole trip as "employees' recreation." This practice of setting up a small company in order to avoid taxes is very common. If we are talking about such a two-person "company," it is a personal matter between husband and wife and not for me to criticize. But as a goal for establishing a real company of any size, it is idiotic.

If one's aim is to set up a company in which the management is disinterested and all the employees are guaranteed to become bored and lazy, I can understand the strategy in theory. The company will be losing money in no time and become a sizable tax write-off. I must confess that, unfashionable as this idea may sound, merely the thought of evading taxes this way bothers me. But this is a secondary question. As someone who has devoted his entire life to learning how to manage a business properly and make it possible for employees to prosper and develop as a result of such management, I am thoroughly disgusted at the thought of corporate directors who would intentionally set up such a "sick" company, trying to escape paying corporate taxes at the sacrifice of other men's lives. Such people are not only unfit to be executives; to my way of thinking, they are little more than "corporate slumlords" providing unfit homes for their staff, and the world would be better off without such selfish pigs.

There is another phenomenon, perhaps not unique to Japan, but certainly very common within our corporate community. That is, when a large company finds itself burdened with excess personnel, it often creates a subsidiary to get rid of the "unwanted fat." Since it is especially difficult for large, white-collar companies to fire people, even when their incompetence has become apparent to all, many firms look for some way to dispose of these unwanted workers. The creation of a new subsidary provides a neat solution, eliminating both unnecessary and unwanted staff without the messy consequences of firings. Many a foreign firm has discovered that the joint venture it established with a reputable Japanese partner is loaded with these "do-nothing" types, some of whom may even hold management positions, for JVs are another classic way to get rid of people who are not wanted in the main company.

In this case, although the new firm is

called a corporation, it is really nothing more than a giant wastebasket. The personnel problems of the parent are simply rounded up and "dumped" into the new company. If you are lucky, there is a fairly good balance between the number of talentless managers sent in to run the show and the number of talentless employees tossed into this "dump." This may seem like a great waste of money to Western eyes, where layoffs and pink slips are common, but in Japan this kind of subsidiary serves a very useful function and is far more common than you would think.

Clearly, in both cases management is acting out of purely selfish motives. Trying to escape taxation and to cut back staff at the head office are poor reasons to start up a new corporation, and the employees of the new subsidiary will not be fooled into thinking otherwise. Those workers who maintain any lingering sense of company identity will never feel loyal to the new firm, and as chances for returning to the parent company dwindle, they will lose any remaining interest in their jobs. Rather than putting out too much effort for their new company, they will think it wiser to simply "put in their time" until retirement. In the end, the company established to evade taxes may become as unmotivated as that set up to "farm out" unwanted personnel. In either case, I believe it is a crime for a large company to waste talent, energy and capital in such a manner.

Big companies vs. small companies

Recently I had the chance to speak with a college student who had been looking for a job. When I advised him to choose a small company rather than a large one, he looked very surprised. He said that he had worked very hard to get into a good university because he wanted to find a job with a big, famous corporation. I was discouraged to realize that he was quite determined and very sure of his goals. I suppose what really upsets me is to think that throughout our country (and probably overseas as well) there are millions of talented and serious young people like this fellow whose only desire is to find security inside a big organization.

When fall sets in, it is common in our country to see college seniors change from their jeans and T-shirts into suits and ties, and begin making the rounds of various companies for interviews. The process is supposed to begin on October 1, but many students jump the gun in their eagerness to make an impression on corporate personnel departments. sooner or later these students obtain offers from a few firms, and then visit their favorite companies once again to line up a job for the new business year (which in Japan begins in April). Some unfor-

tunate students must continue to seek employment even after this. The young man I met was
one of these. He had recently been for interviews at Toyota, Canon and NEC. I asked him
why he had decided to visit these three giant
manufacturing firms, which have nothing in
common save for the scale of their businesses.
He gave me several reasons, but in the end it
became clear that the underlying appeal of these
firms was simply their size and reputations. If he
could just land a job with one of them, he said,
he would be free from worry about his future.

I cannot agree with this way of thinking,
and I told him so straight away. He seemed like
a bright enough fellow, so I'm sure he ignored
my advice and went on to find an entry-level
position at some large firm. But I was quite
serious in advising him not to follow this path.
Everyone thinks a big company is more stable,
just as this student did. They believe that if one
is employed by a large and well-known company, one's livelihood and future happiness are
secured. To some degree this is true, at least in
Japan, where layoffs from big companies are all
but unheard of. Still, I believe my advice is well-
founded. A large company may appear strong
and vital, but all too often it is nothing more
than a comfortable trap. Sure, they will guarantee your salary for the next forty years, but only
if you are willing to give up your freedom and
any sense of creativity you might have had. For

the dull and unmotivated, I can see some advantages in this, but for a promising young university student who could make valuable contributions to our world if given freedom, direction and encouragement, it is a sad waste of talent. I may sound overly extreme in saying this, but I absolutely believe this is true. I have done business with many giant companies and know many employees at such firms, and I know very well what happens to individuals once they become part of such huge organizations.

Japan's corporate giants are the envy of much of the commercial world these days. Yet, there is not a doubt in my mind that their power will peak and they will go into decline sooner or later. It may happen ten years from now, or twenty, or thirty, but they are doomed to fail in the end. Of course, everything comes to an end sooner or later, but as far as a company is concerned, the larger it becomes, the faster it will fall. Why? Because as it grows ever more obese, it becomes sluggish and conservative and must compensate for its lack of drive by using its size and financial clout to achieve results. This is the beginning of the end.

It is widely accepted as a normal goal for a company to grow both big and internally strong. However, history clearly shows that such cases are extremely rare. In most cases, as a company grows larger it becomes weaker internally, more of a bureaucracy and less a strong competitor. An old Japanese proverb says, "A mountain is not admirable just because it is lofty." The same holds true for a large company. Ideally, a company should be armed with bold, dedicated and vigorous employees from the bottom to the top of its organization. I know very few companies that fit that description, but among those that do, I am hard put to think of a single large corporation.

It is often pointed out that in Japan the years one spends in college are not so academically strenuous as those in the U.S. or Europe, and students who study overseas always comment on this when returning to university in Japan. But if their collegiate education is not so fulfilling, why do our best and brightest work so extremely hard to get into the top universities? Simply because they want to find employment with well-known companies. They obviously see these giant organizations as symbols of prestige, job security and stability. To the young person setting out on a new career, getting into a big firm looks like a meal ticket for life. And once their goal is achieved, many of them feel that somehow they have risen in stature and become famous just because they now work for a famous company. They think their life's problems are solved and they have only to show up every day and do as they are told until retirement comes. And is that so bad? After all, they won't have to get their hands dirty or their shirts sweaty; they won't have to show respect to some particularly nasty client or bow to those whom they dislike—just sit at a desk for a certain number of hours every day, do their work and go home.

But are these people, bright though they are according to our university entrance exams, really the best our country has to offer? Are the companies they revere so laudable merely because they appear on the stock pages of our papers and are reported about on television? Recently we have seen scandals involving even the biggest and most respected firms, scandals that have severely hurt not only the pride of the firms' employees but their business performance as well. In Japan and the U.S. we have seen large multinational companies sustain serious losses due to unforeseeable factors such as illegal trading, political scandals, industrial accidents and so on. Who is to say that an even greater scandal is not awaiting the big and well-established companies these young men rush to enter? Any of a dozen unforeseen circumstances could easily bring down the power and glory of a giant firm in less than a year. And so often these problems themselves are rooted in the firm's lack of control over its own internal operations—again, a clear sign that a company, no matter how profitable, has grown too big.

Even something as simple as a shift in business conditions can ruin a firm that we all revered as invincible only a short time ago. In Japan we have only to look at some of the giant steel or shipbuilding companies to see how clearly this message is written. In the U.S. as well there are giant firms that have been struck a mortal blow by circumstances out of their control and lost the power to control their own destinies. What of the employees in these firms? Perhaps many of those who are now looking for a "safe" firm to move to originally joined the company because of its size, prestige and appearance of stability.

If one is employed by a smaller firm, on the other hand, there are far fewer guarantees. Life is less secure and one has to make an effort every day. Undoubtedly, one must work harder and bow one's head more often. In some jobs you have to use your head, not simply bow it— since there are fewer people to share responsibility, you must use your brains, think for yourself and be creative. In other jobs you have to use your muscles more—get your hands dirty and your shirt soaked with sweat. In both cases you must be constantly thinking of your customers: doing good work for the benefit of people whom you will never see and being polite at all times to those you do see. But is this such a demeaning and discouraging prospect? I don't think so. To me the true meaning of work is to do one's job the very best one can, whether with a computer or a drill press, and go home proud of what you have accomplished.

This applies not only to lower-level employees but to managers as well. The manager of a small firm in Japan is expected to bow more deeply and more often to his clients than his subordinates do. He must bear ultimate responsibility for the fate of each business relationship, be the "face" of his company and, no matter how dire circumstances may become, always look confident and be a rock for his staff to cling to. That is the burden of his position, and any man who can't handle it should step aside and make way for someone who can.

I regret to say that I see more and more young men from good colleges who have no desire to know the meaning of work. They seem to feel privileged to keep their hands clean and live lives of comparative ease. Often I think how fortunate I am that my companies do not attract such men. What would happen if we were to become so big and famous that we attracted a lot of applicants fresh from the top universities? I am not saying that all these young people are lazy or stuck-up; but I am convinced that many if not most of them are immature, far too concerned with themselves and their own ideas of success. My companies are places for work to be done, not babysitting services. There are lots of other places for these bright young people to go.

The other day a young representative of a famous Japanese bank came to see me on business. His firm was established about three hundred years ago and is well known for its skillful management and high-class image. The young man, who had just graduated from Tokyo University (the most prestigious school in Japan), was quite direct, not wasting time with pleasantries, and said rather brusquely, "You don't do much business with our bank, do you? If you did, I'm sure you could get a better line of credit."

I was stunned. I don't know how bankers may act in other countries, but in Japan the banks are highly esteemed and their employees are expected to be the "gentlemen of commerce." Obviously this young man's credentials were impeccable, yet his manner suggested a young gangster more than an elite businessman.

I said to him as gently as possible, "If the founder of your bank were to walk in here right now, he would first bow very deeply. Then he would say how grateful he was for my patronage to date. He would then inquire about my health, my family and the state of my business. Lastly, he would ask me please to continue to favor the bank with my patronage and say that if there was any way he could be of service, please call upon him personally. In time, as a result of his kindness and solicitous attitude, I might very well increase the size and variety of my dealings with the bank. . . . How sad it makes me to see that times have changed so." The young man seemed unable to reply. Fortunately for him, no reply was necessary. I offered him some tea and we chatted about nothing of consequence for a short time. He excused himself more politely than he had come in, and I have not seen him since.

It is a sad truth that as a company grows, men like this increase. There is no relationship (unless it is an inverse one) between a firm's being big and famous and its being staffed by capable people. My own policy is not to drive away even graduates of Tokyo University if they are prepared to work and behave like adults. If they seek pride in their company, let them first have pride in their own work and show respect towards others.

One day, I was reading a book on anthropology and came across a chapter about schools. Children attending big schools, it said, normally do not have to do as much work as those in small schools. For example, at a small school the children are supposed to perform such tasks as erasing blackboards, cleaning the room, watering the plants and so on because everyone in the school is responsible for its upkeep. In contrast, children at a big school are often freed from such tasks, which become the duties of the custodial staff. Yet, children who are required to assume various responsibilities and perform such tasks at school seem to acquire habits at an early age that will make them better citizens. In the same way, a small company gives each worker greater responsibilities and more of a sense that he or she plays an important role in the organization as a whole. I have seen time and again how this helps to increase people's capacity to perform.

In Japan, it is a popular practice for companies to hold frequent study sessions or seminars for their workers. The companies incur great expense to pay for lectures on "total quality control" or similar subjects. This has always seemed to me to be a waste of money. What can a TQC seminar teach the employees of a big company? An executive of a big firm once told me that, despite the cost and the inconvenience of running regular training programs, the firm's seminars weren't really very effective. I'm afraid I said something glib like "Well, what did you expect?" but I couldn't help it. A small company is constantly performing quality control and constantly looking for ways to improve its operation. If it stops doing so, even for a month or two, the sales figures will tell the story. Looking at it another way, if it were your job to monitor quality control and to make sure that every worker was exerting his best efforts, where do you think you could best do that—in a firm with thousands of employees or one with just a hundred or so? I have nothing against productivity seminars in principle, but isn't it better simply not to need them?

In 1983 I published (at my own expense) a book in which I told the history of my family and the development of the Taiyo Group companies. It tells how my family has lived through difficult times over three generations, and I flatter myself that I did a reasonably good job in writing it. I was reviewed favorably by a famous critic, and as a result, letters and telephone calls poured into our office from all over the country requesting a copy. The rush of orders pleased me very much. However, as I had not given it to a publishing company, I had to ask callers to pay for it directly.

One day I had a call from one of the largest companies in Japan, a giant steel producer in Kyushu. I wondered who in such a world-famous company wanted to read such a trivial book written by the head of a small manufacturing company. "Thank you for your interest in my book," I said to the secretary over the phone. "I'll ship you a copy immediately. It's only a few dollars, so could you please send me a check to cover the cost plus postage?" To my surprise, she said, "Mr. Sakai, we are a big company. We always send money directly by electronic bank transfer. Please invoice us at your earliest convenience for the book plus the shipping charges." I was a bit taken aback for a moment, but then realized that of course our simple way of paying a small bill would be inappropriate for a mammoth corporation. I forwarded a copy of my book to the company with a bill and a note of appreciation for their inquiry.

About a month passed, and I had another call from the same secretary. I had already forgotten about our previous conversation. "I'm sorry, Mr. Sakai, but your official company seal is not stamped on the invoice. Please re-invoice us as soon as possible, and don't forget the seal." I did as she asked. In a few days she called again. In order to make the transfer at the bank, she explained, she had to write my name using the phonetic Japanese alphabet rather than the normal Sino-Japanese characters with which my name appears on the invoice. While my family name is easy to read, she did not know how to read my first name, she said, and so could I please tell her how to read it correctly so that she could put through the paperwork for the bank transfer? I could not help laughing out loud. The company she was working for was one of the biggest firms in Japan and a world leader in its industry. No doubt her parents were proud that their daughter was employed at such an internationally renowned corporation. But what was she doing at the company? My book cost only six dollars. Had she or her employer merely sent me a check, she could have completed the transaction in two minutes; instead, she was wasting valuable company time to ask me how to spell my name, and running up long-distance phone charges worth several times the cost of my book.

Trivial as this example may be, I think every manager of a large company must nod his head and say to himself, "You don't know the half of it." Company time, company facilities and company funds exist to be wasted. Workers feel it is a little unwritten "bonus" tacked on to their salaries. It may be of some interest to know that this particular company has since fallen on hard times. While I was genuinely saddened to hear this, as you can imagine, I was not shocked. The company suffers from "obesity," and my conversation with the secretary was just a brief glimpse at the bureaucratic fat behind the prestigious image of this giant firm. For the next several weeks "We're a big company" was a popular joke in my office.

The other day I came across a newspaper article that I found depressing, all the more so because it happened to involve my own countrymen. A large project had been announced in an oil-producing country. More than ten huge companies from the United States, England, France and Japan had raced to that country and were trying frantically to secure the contract. In order to make the winning bid, the Japanese company had obviously invested a large sum of money (although in exactly what endeavors was not specified). According to the newspaper, even if the Japanese company should win the contract, its profit would be negligible, as it has already spent too much money on behind-the-scenes political maneuvering and other expenses. If it does not win, all this expense simply goes down the drain.

When I read things like this I cannot help but see in my mind a picture of enormous dinosaurs fighting each other for the last food on earth. It is all right for a living thing to feed on its environment and to grow bigger. But when it becomes too big that it cannot easily adapt itself to changes in the environment, it begins to fight with its rivals even though the gains may be meager compared to the struggle to obtain them. When this begins to happen, we know that the dinosaurs' days are numbered.

I use the analogy of dinosaurs for a reason. I believe that a company is like a living organism. It can be healthy or frail, big or small, growing or dying. Yet it is very much alive; its component parts interact like organs in a body and the entity itself must interact with its environment in order to survive. Like the dinosaurs, large corporations and conglomerates have grown to enormous size, awesome and powerful, masters of the world. However, as they grow they find they need more and more "nourishment" to stay alive. Any company, if not held in check by external conditions or internal policies, will normally grow and keep growing. When it was small it was easy to survive, for it required relatively little to sustain its existence. In some cases, smaller entities can live off of big ones quite comfortably. As long as the bigger entities are healthy, that is. Once it has grown very big, however, a giant organization changes and begins to lose its ability to adapt to its environment. When that happens, it may try to do what the dinosaurs could not: that is, to actually change its environment rather than adapt to it (by influencing government decisions, for example), but by this point its ultimate end is already written.

In contrast, smaller entities can maintain their existence far more easily. Because what they lack in sheer size and power is more than compensated for in agility and adaptability, there is a much greater chance that the smaller ones will survive long after the giants have perished. Because a company is a living organism, the key to its survival is to stay healthy, to be fit and trim, ready to compete and ready to adapt if its business environment begins to change. Growth is normal and is desirable, but *it is essential to control growth* or the company will ultimately suffer.

The most vital question, then, for any company that is healthy, growing and working hard to expand its operations and increase its profits is "How can we achieve controlled growth?"

The answer is simple: by dividing the company while it is still energetic and vital, thus creating a new firm fired up with the energy of youth and an older firm revitalized by slimming down its operations and personnel. Most importantly, this will create dozens, perhaps hundreds, of promotions or new positions in both firms, meaning that a large percentage of the staff in both companies will suddenly be faced with new responsibilities and new challenges in their jobs. Nothing I know of will better motivate people and nothing will light a fire under a company more than this.

If company division is carried out properly, at least one of these firms will develop rapidly in the next few years and become a stronger, more dynamic company than anyone expected. How do you reward a firm that is growing quickly and showing tremendous potential for the future? Divide it.

I know some will say, "Why kill a firm just when it is starting to mature?" but they are missing the point. Company division doesn't "kill" anything, except perhaps the feeling that you can sit around and do nothing and still make money. Company division taps the most basic energy that exists in every successful enterprise. Its growth potential is not cut short. Just the opposite. *Bunsha* releases this energy, which is the real source of corporate strength, to make an old company new and a new company grow.

How do I divide my companies?

When a company has become stable and is moving on a steady expansion course, I think it should begin to think seriously about division. Usually this is just the point at which the executives are feeling that they can relax a bit. Revenues are increasing, new staff are coming on board and the problems that crop up are not the kind that threaten the firm's existence. Yet this is precisely where the danger lies. Of course I want my managers to be able to relax, and it is important for them to be models for other employees, demonstrating that people should enjoy their work, not simply do it so that it gets done. But when the the challenge of developing the company begins to wane, it's time for a change. I do not have in mind a target level of annual sales, a certain growth rate, a number of personnel or any other yardstick by which to determine that a company is ripe for division. A good manager knows when his company is healthy, sound and growing, and he knows when it is nearing its peak of performance in terms of size vs. efficiency. When that time comes—or, hopefully, even a little before—he should have the courage to defy the conventional "bigger is better" wisdom and divide his company.

The decision to divide may be agonizing the first time, but once you have made it, the process moves along with a life of its own. You pick a capable president to lead the new firm, give him enough start-up capital to keep his head above water for a while and let him decide what he needs in the way of staff and equipment. Then, if you are like me, you will lose sleep worrying about two companies instead of one for a period of time, but this will not last. Before long you will realize that you have made the right choice in selecting a president, and his good sense will guide it to ultimate success. When both firms are stable and growing, you will sleep well again.

If this new president is the heart of the company, his employees are the lifeblood that animates it. Thus, I give the new president a free hand to recruit his favorite colleagues from inside our corporate group as well as to solicit men from outside our group to join his new venture. Of course, the loss of some key person on our side is also hard to accept, and at first I can't help wanting to say, "Hey, you can't take Takahashi—he's the only guy in Accounting who can add!" But I have come to realize the importance of giving the new president the benefit of trusted friends and associates to work with.

As I have just noted, I view a company as an organic whole, and as such, a body that has certain needs and limitations. The corporation, like a human being, must not become sedentary or put on excess fat: too much stress will hurt it, but without some stress it will not grow. Thus, when I now see some key personnel being spirited off to one of our new companies, I feel as if our firm is giving blood. When a great deal is removed, you might feel dizzy, perhaps even lose the ability to function properly for a short while. But in time the missing blood is replaced from within: the body responds to the situation and reproduces what is lost. No matter how frequently the blood is drawn from a company, it will grow healthy and strong again. And of course the new company will benefit from the donation, growing strong and healthy with the energy and experience of its staff. Perhaps in a few years it, too, will need to give blood to help its own offspring come to life.

Picking the right person

Perhaps the single most important factor in dividing a company is to select a capable leader to guide the new firm. Just like a locomotive pulling a train, the new chief executive must be the force that pulls the new company together and gets it rolling in the right direction. To divide a company does not mean simply splitting your own company in two with a trusted associate assuming half of the management burden. It means establishing a new and independent company. The newly appointed manager is not a hired president; he is the creator of a wholly new enterprise. If the right man is chosen in the first place, the success of the company almost always follows as a matter of course.

My own philosophy is to pick the right man, give him all the support I can and then get out of his way and let him do his job. Once I've entrusted him with the responsibilities of being a manager, I don't interfere in his management decisions, no matter how tempted I may be to butt in. He must develop his own management style with his co-workers. The last thing he needs is meddling from an outsider. If this sounds nerve-wracking for the person who selected him, I assure you, it is. Every time. But that's part of *bunsha*.

However small the new firm may be, I insist that it should have its own full complement of departments just as any other company would. Some people question this system, asking why it is necessary to have, for example, separate personnel, accounting, legal and finance departments when the new company and its "parent" are like brothers. Critics are quick to point out that direct control by the parent company is far more efficient and economical, especially when the new company is just starting up. However, efficiency and economy are not always the most important factors in providing for the success of a new enterprise. Again, experience has taught me that human beings respond positively to being completely entrusted with a certain task. "Which is preferable," I asked a manager of another company who questioned me on this point, "to have your targets or production quotas determined by someone 'up above' or to set them yourself? To have materials assigned by an outside party or to purchase them yourself?" He agreed with me, but still couldn't help feeling that somehow central control was more efficient. I can easily understand this viewpoint, as I, too, believed it once. But I have since learned that the real meaning of efficiency is not always to be found in an accountant's ledger.

One more point: while centralization may be more effective for cost reduction, it also has a serious defect. Centralization limits information gathering. This is an age of information, not only from electronic media, but from person-to-person contact, and perhaps this latter is even more important than it used to be. If each company in a group has one person in charge of purchasing and another responsible for funding, and so on, their combined information network will be greater than that of any single company and will ultimately prove beneficial to all the firms in the group.

Returning to the new leader of a divided company: obviously, it is important to find someone who is confident, energetic and full of drive. However, a man who appears unassuming on the surface sometimes turns out to be full of energy. Therefore, I do not rely solely on appearances or past accomplishments when evaluating a man for this most important task. I make it a rule to use my intuition. Not very objective, you might say, but effective nonetheless. In the past thirty years I have seldom made a major mistake in this respect. Am I an unusually good judge of men? No, I don't think so. Any man who runs a successful company has his share of intuition, and must rely on it as much as on any empirical form of decision-making. My only advice to the president faced with the painful task of entrusting a new business venture to one man is to trust his own intuition first.

When your intuition tells you to pick a man whose appearance or credentials don't seem quite up to the job, you will often see the qualities that your "hunch" told you were hiding beneath the surface brought out much faster than you expected. When the new president is exposed to the realities of running his own company, he will mature quickly, surprising everyone around him, sometimes even the man who took a chance in selecting him. I find it especially gratifying to see a person's hidden talent emerging from deep inside. Like a man who cannot swim a stroke who is suddenly dropped in the ocean, the new president finds himself overwhelmed by the enormity of his task. But soon enough he finds that he is not going to drown, he gets his bearings and he sets off towards dry land.

Perhaps this helps to clarify what I was saying before. I've mentioned that it is important to pick the right man for the job, and that intuition plays a big part in that. But it occurs to me I might have given the impression that this "right man" is a sharp young manager in your firm just waiting to be given the nod to assume his predestined role as president of a new firm. This is usually far from the case.

I believe one must gain first-hand experience in order to master any skill. A how-to program on TV cannot teach you, nor can reading a text on the subject. All the books ever written about management won't make anyone a good manager. In short, we only learn by doing. Therefore, I don't believe that the "right" man can be selected for the "right" position from the very beginning. Only God can put a person in the position that is best designed for him from the start, knowing that he will ripen to the job at hand because it is his destiny. In my experience, most people prove their real talents only in the face of circumstances they don't anticipate. They rise to a challenge and become something greater than they or anyone else believed possible. It is then that a man who initially looked less than ideal puts forth his hidden ability. This is why I say credentials are not the most important consideration and only intuition can lead you to a man who may be right for the job. But you never know for sure; *bunsha* is always a gamble.

In short, my system does not rest as much on choosing talented people as on drawing hidden talent from them. The chosen leader may have witnessed his former boss raising capital, hiring staff, negotiating with various parties and so on, but did he ever attempt any of these challenges himself? Of course not. But now he is the boss. Every problem a new company could possibly face awaits his decision. There is no time for idling. He is not responsible to those above him, but to those below him who have faith that he will not let the company fail. A man leading others must have a strong sense of duty. At times the strain of his responsibilities may prove nearly unbearable, but he will triumph, partly because of this sense of duty, and partly because his own inner strength begins to flow when he faces an impossible situation. And, strange as it may sound to some, witnessing this process has been the single biggest reward I have gained personally from dividing my companies.

I sometimes think of myself as an explorer, an archaeologist continually seeking to rediscover man's hidden qualities. As I said before, dividing a company is always a gamble, and I, too, must face the uncertainties of the new company's maiden voyage. Confident as I am in my choice of a new president, my stomach always feels as if we're on the verge of a shipwreck. I know too well how many problems a small company must face and the kind of unexpected crises that befall it almost daily. However, it is this danger that kindles the spirit of the new leader. It is said that perfectly average people gain the strength and courage of ten when fire threatens their homes. Occasionally I think of myself as an arsonist who sets fires in the hearts of promising young men in the hope of calling forward their deeply hidden instincts to rise above themselves. Once this spirit is kindled, there is little to worry about. All I have to do is to prevent intruders from quenching it.

Brave, capable men are not born: they rise to meet a challenge. Without a crisis there is no need for a hero. And yet, the very attraction of a big company to most people is its stability and lack of turbulence, the very things which guarantee that its employees will lack drive. In a small, recently divided company, the new leader must be a fighter of sorts, because he has to start from scratch. The managers must become real leaders, and every man and woman in the company must put forth greater efforts. This makes for a better working environment for everyone. This is why I divide my companies.

Does this whole system sound completely fanciful? I don't think so. Still, you may ask, don't I occasionally have second thoughts? My answer is a simple and unqualified "No." I have only one regret, and that is that I did not start this system many years earlier. The fiscal soundness of the companies I have created more than satisfies our accountants, and the bright faces I see in our offices and the positive atmosphere I feel in our plants tell me time and again that we made the right choice. This is all the proof I need that *bunsha* is the key to building a strong, dynamic group of companies that will both prosper as businesses and enrich the lives of their employees.

GOOD MANAGERS ARE
GOOD LEADERS

It would be nice if all our jobs could be exciting and interesting all the time. Unfortunately, they cannot. It is an inescapable fact that some kinds of work are less stimulating than others, and the inherent danger of a monotonous job is not just the loss of efficiency but the loss of an employee's spirit. As people become familiar with a certain job, especially a routine one, they gradually lose interest in their work. It becomes too easy; they can do it with their eyes closed, they say, and if we're not careful, they will. When the challenge of the job disappears, it is only natural to relax and, before long, to stop paying attention to the work itself. But a wise manager is sensitive to this and knows how to stimulate his employees. He not only gives his people vacations, but changes work assignments occasionally. He may rotate them within the section, exchange personnel with another section, even give them a two-week "in-company vacation" in another division when possible.

One of the fundamental principles of *bunsha* is the idea that "responsibility motivates." Thus, managers in my companies are not afraid to divide even small groups into smaller groups. I have seen a manager take a section of ten people and divide it in two, making one employee in each sub-section responsible for the work of that unit. The managers also keep tabs on what other sections are doing; if one group is outstanding, for example, a manager in another section may say to his people, "Why don't you take the morning and go find out what they're doing over there? They must have something on the ball; let's find out what it is!" Outside observers sometimes comment that this system seems wasteful of valuable work time. I couldn't disagree more. Our system is designed to stimulate people at all levels in a company.

Many managers feel it is their job to create an atmosphere where employees can work. Idiots! It is the responsibility of the managers to create an environment in which employees will be encouraged to work. Without enthusiasm, how can one be expected to perform? I say to my managers, "Experiment! Don't be limited by what you've seen before, either here or in other firms. Be creative!" The creative manager may even go out of his way to shock his employees, to do or say things to wake them up and make them look at their jobs afresh. He inspires them and leads them, and they respond, because every good manager is at heart a good leader.

All levels of managers, down to the section chiefs, must focus as much attention as possible on the problem of cultivating a good company atmosphere. I am convinced that companies which do not provide a pleasant and interesting working environment will sooner or later fail. Of course, this alone is not sufficient: a fitting salary is also necessary. In general, a company must adopt an attitude whereby it rewards employees not merely for their labor but for satisfying customers, for that is actually what they are doing, regardless of what kind of business the firm is engaged in or where in the organization each individual is working. The employee must be made to feel that his or her efforts are directly connected to the success of the organization (and, needless to say, this becomes more difficult as the organization gets larger). Managers should thus show sincere appreciation to each employee for his or her work. I believe that managers who do not develop this attitude should be relieved of their positions.

The good manager knows that his employees work best in a free atmosphere. They do not want to feel forced or interfered with. Constant nagging will only serve to discourage them. A good leader must try to discover each individual's merit, and give each one as much discretion as possible. Only then will they give their best efforts consistently. To put it another way, people must be allowed to express their creativity somehow on the job and thus derive pleasure from their work. By this I mean an "active" rather than a "passive" pleasure, the pleasure of doing rather than of being entertained. Putting a television set in the office will entertain, and some might even say it improves the working environment, but this is not what

I'm talking about. What should be sought after is an attitude of willingness to participate and to exert creativity. The working environment must promote creative involvement. I don't care how routine a job may look: when it is performed by a human being there is always room for some kind of individual involvement. Every form filled out, every document filed away, every phone call answered, every rivet set, every nail driven, every truck unloaded, is done by a human being, not a robot. It may be done well or done poorly, but this is the result of individual action, and thus it is a creation. *Give each person in your company the feeling that he or she is creating something and is uniquely responsible for that creation, and you will truly be a success as a manager.*

Recently I heard an interesting story about athletic training. A person who undertakes serious training of his own free will usually develop more powerful lungs and muscles than a person forced to do so. Clearly, one's own desire to perform well can be a better manager than any form of external supervision. Unfortunately, although we live in a free society which extols our individual rights, excessive supervision has become commonplace. Coaches interfere with the players not only in their training but in their private lives as well. For example, Japanese athletes who participated in the Los Angeles Olympics were not allowed to leave their camp without permission from their coaches. What nonsense! Why did the coaches treat these athletes like children? Why let them go all the way to Los Angeles, but not allow them to walk around freely? A wrestler was nearly sent back to Japan for breaking one of the coaches' restrictions. What was his offense? He secretly brought a camera and took some photographs on the day of the opening parade. His coach caught him and made him write a letter of apology to the Olympic Committee. Needless to say, they were at a loss as to how to deal with the issue as many other foreign athletes had also taken pictures of the ceremony and none of their coaches made them write a letter of apology. It later turned out that this same wrestler won a gold medal. Perhaps, we at home thought on reading of this, our other athletes did not win medals because they were so completely stifled by their coaches' obsession with strict control.

A man named Yuji Matsuo leads the strongest rugby team in Japan. He is often asked about the secret of maintaining his team's performance at such a consistently high level. "You must be giving them special training and very strenuous workouts," reporters say to him. "Tell us a little about your method." Mr. Matsuo invariably replies, "Sorry, but I don't have a special method. And I don't give them particularly hard workouts. Our training program is just like that of any other team." When pressed to explain why his men perform so well if their training regimen is so ordinary, Matsuo can only say that his own attitude towards the players may be a bit unusual: "I always aim at drawing their natural strength from them. I respect each member's humanity." Matsuo stated that a really tough three-hour practice cannot produce better results than a thirty-minute intensive training that meets the players' own desires to keep in top shape.

His words echoed in my head for days, for they apply just as well to business management. Too many managers like to control their workers like the Japanese coaches at the Olympics. "We run a tight ship," they say, but they are the ones limiting the ship's progress. What does anyone feel if forced to work under this type of domineering manager? Far from being encouraged, one would soon become disillusioned and lose both the desire and the ability to perform well.

A good manager must also treat his employees with strict fairness. Of course it is important for employees to work enthusiastically, but this implies that they are contributing to the firm's profits. A firm must be in the black, otherwise neither the executives nor the employees can benefit. If an employee makes a serious error which may lead to losses or bankruptcy, the manager must deal with this individual quickly and effectively, regardless of his position or one's personal feelings. Compassion for subordinates is desirable, but excessive tolerance of their mastakes is a critical error. A good manager will not overlook a serious mistake made by his men, but will be both strict and fair in his treatment.

The daily operations of a company are the fruit of creative efforts and hard work. Those who have a negative view of life or feel forced to work against their will cannot produce great results because their creativity is suppressed. Thus, a good manager is the essential transformer that changes a sterile company environment into a place in which human beings can grow. He creates a positive working environment, and his co-workers respond in the most positive way, by achieving their leader's goals to the best of their ability. Every manager at every level should remember this. If his employees seem unmotivated, lethargic or routinized, it is because the most important element is missing from their working environment. It is not a TV or a coffee machine, nor a new slogan to hang on the wall. It is simply the "spark" that should make that office a good place to work—the catalyst that only a good manager can supply.

In a famous Chinese book of strategy there is a saying, "Take care of your men as you would your own children, and they will follow you down into the deepest valley. Love them as your own children, and they will gladly die for you." A leader should treat his subordinates with compassion and consideration, and they will respond in kind with unswerving loyalty. They will not shrink from any challenge or crisis, and will always be prepared to make sacrifices for him. A man who cannot instill this feeling in his subordinates is not an effective manager and should never be allowed to run a company.

In addition to this spirit of compassion, a good leader must be able to instill a positive attitude in his employees at all levels, allowing each to do his best in accordance with his or her ability. A manager who has no need to "live in the clouds" of executive suites can be a powerful influence his employees. He can encourage them to develop their individual potential and can help them to maintain interest in their work. He shows his regard for their abilities by trusting them completely, and if something prevents them from executing their duties, he changes things so that they can succeed.

A good leader makes his fellow workers cheerful. His presence itself makes them feel at ease. We say that some men are born optimists, but many men feel that the optimism and cheerfulness they had in their youth has disappeared by the time they have become managers. "What a lot of nonsense," I say, and I speak from experience because I am one such "self-made optimist." Everyone who knows me says that I am jovial and easy-going, and they all think I was born both cheerful and optimistic. If only they knew! In fact, I was terribly serious and even depressed when I was younger. I felt the burden of being a young president with too little experience. I was burning with desire to make my firm the best in Japan, and the pressure of my responsibilities weighed on me like a heavy stone around my neck. Fortunately, I was helped by my good friend, Hiroshi, who awakened me to the need to be a model for my workers, not just by being responsible and diligent, but also by being cheerful and positive no matter what the situation. I am forever indebted to him for so many contributions, all of which helped to make my business a success, and yet this simple piece of advice is one of the most important things he ever did for me.

A manager is always on display. If he tries to hide in his office all the time and cut himself off from his workers, he might as well resign, for he has lost the ability to manage. But all the time that he is visible to his employees, whether showing clients around, joking with his workers, eating lunch with his staff, even just standing in the elevator or walking through the building, he must remember that he is being watched. Not consciously, perhaps, but every person in the company pays attention to how he looks, how he sounds. Employees in any company are always trying to read the boss's face and the tone of his voice on the telephone. Not only will they react to his mood, particularly if he is angry or depressed, but they will also take it as a sign of difficulties facing the firm, and this can only have a negative impact on their performance. When I was president of Taiyo Industries, I obviously had many subordinates. If I was in low spirits, they couldn't help but notice and be affected by my negative feelings. On the other hand, if I was optimistic, they naturally tended to share in my optimism. Thanks to Hiroshi's advice, I decided that a gloomy atmosphere did not become my company, and that I was going to do everything possible to be more positive. From then on I made a conscious effort to look and act like a man enjoying life.

I began to exchange jokes with my fellow workers and laughed a lot. Whenever I found a worker looking a little down, I'd tap him on the shoulder and say, "Cheer up! You're doing a good job. Keep it up—I'm proud of your work." By and by, I found that this was far more effective than always finding fault with them. "Take it easy!" I'd say to another. "We've got to save a little energy for the party on Saturday." In this way my own determination to act more cheerful was a big factor in changing my attitude towards work. And, of course, the prosperity of the company helped to give me a cheerful disposition. As the years went by, I became more and more light-hearted, even when things were not going well, for I had learned the truth of having an unshakable positive attitude. Although some people say that hardships make men stubborn and old, they had just the opposite effect on me.

A good leader is always seeking out and making preparations to enter a new market. The fate of a company depends on its chief executive's efforts and planning. If he constantly endeavors to find new frontiers for his firm, it will endure. One can never be too much on guard in this highly competitive world. Even if one's firm is at its zenith and shows tremendous profits, it may go bankrupt at any time. It is much easier to predict the weather than to predict profits in the next business term. Therefore, a good manager is always on his guard against any conceivable disaster.

A good leader will get along easily with people around him, sometimes setting aside time to go out and socialize with his employees. He knows that spending time with people and enjoying their company is good for everyone concerned, and that means it is good for business as well. In terms of making friends, though, he must be careful. A man who is not capable of judging other people well is not a top-class executive. Such individuals often make friends with people of questionable integrity. Confucius once said that one of the most important things in life is to be able to read a friend's face well. He was absolutely right. The number of people one meets in a lifetime is limited, as is our lifespan. To establish friendship with people of dubious character is merely a great waste of time. Thus, a good manager should be careful to prevent himself from falling into adverse relationships, for he will be judged by the company he keeps. A man who does not have a keen insight into human nature and motivation cannot become a good leader.

There are some managers who are very diligent, yet do not know how to lead their employees. Isn't it a shame for a man to be so greatly absorbed in his own work that he neglects his subordinates? He should try to make his policies understood and never become weary of instilling his thoughts and ideas into those working for him. If he believes that he can influence others through silent diligence, he is mistaken. They will never understand what he expects from them unless he articulates those expectations each time the occasion arises.

If a manager intends to earn their respect, he would do well to play down his own contributions and instead praise the efforts of his subordinates. I am proud of myself as a practitioner of good business management. I like to think I have become a connoisseur of men as well. These days I have many visitors who come to discuss all sorts of business-related problems,

and I also travel frequently to stay in touch with
our employees and to meet with people in various fields of endeavor. It is said that as a paint-
er keeps gazing at landscapes, he comes to
notice shadows, colors and features that ordinary people fail to see. In this way, when I sit
face to face with my guests or visitors, I believe
I can see some of what is hidden inside. Confucius probably meant this when he talked about
"reading your friend's face."

I mentioned before that a good leader is
compassionate, but a man who bestows too
much compassion upon his employees may
bring the company to ruin. Nothing is as difficult for the Japanese as firing employees who
have been faithful and rendered service to the
company. We are often too compassionate to
sever connections with our friends, and I must
confess, it is one of our weak points. Once in a
while, however, a serious situation arises in
which one must take a firm stand or face the
most serious of consequences. At such a time,
the president must discharge people for the sake
of the company, even if he feels as if he is stab-
bing himself to do so. Refusing to act, either
out of compassion or fear, does not solve the
problem.

There is a story well known in Japan of a
Chinese lord in the 4th century B.C. who had
to fight against a much stronger enemy. His
small but loyal army had taken up an advan-

tageous position on a river bank when the enemy's forces appeared on the far side and began
to wade toward them. The lord's military advisors counselled an immediate attack, but he
held them back, saying, "A gentleman should
not wound the injured or the aged; how can I
then attack an unprepared enemy?" When the
enemy had forded the river and taken their
stance, he commanded his men to attack, but
the outcome had already been decided, and his
small army was decimated. The lord acted fairly
and with compassion. He did not kill or wound
his enemy's unprepared troops, which we might
say is commendable, but as a result his men
were slaughtered. Were they not in fact killed
by their own lord, for whom they died need-
lessly?

It is often said that business is a sort of
war as well. A company president, like a com-
mander, is required to choose the most appropriate course for his company, and sometimes
this is not easy. But a man who cannot do what
is necessary to save his firm had best resign
immediately. I sometimes see the head of a
small firm who has yielded to pressure from
large companies (who remind me of the superior forces with whom we must sometimes con-
tend). He has forgotten that business is a war,
and if we lose, those whom we have fought so
hard to help will lose also. A president must
remember that indecision, short-sightedness or

avarice on his part may ultimately prove fatal to his firm.

Most importantly, a good manager must always be in tune with his customers' needs. My companies are mostly manufacturing firms, so our relations with our customers are clearly tied to our products, but this axiom is just as true in any other kind of business. Whatever product, service or activity you represent, your customers must feel that you are thinking of their success first and your own second. This is such a fundamental point in running a business that it seems totally obvious to me, and yet I am surprised to see how many firms forget it, sometimes even becoming arrogant with the people with whom they do business.

In each factory of the Taiyo Group there is a sign on the wall: "Are our customers *completely* satisfied?" Our managers make sure that every new worker understands that this is not just some cute saying we thought would look good on the wall. Our customers are vital to our business; we must consider their interests first, last and in between. What is really good for them? What do they want? What will they be looking for in the future? When I talk to executives of other companies who boast of having "squeezed" a customer on price or short-changed him just a little on quantity, quality or delivery schedule just to make a little extra profit, I can only shake my head in disbelief. How long do these fools expect to stay in business?

Years ago when our companies first exhibited the kind of success that we now take for granted, people would ask me, "What is the secret of your group?" I could only answer, "We take care of our customers and they take care of us." Of course, there are many aspects to making your business a success, but in one sense it all boils down to establishing strong relationships with the people who keep you in business. It takes a very long time to win a customer's confidence, and it can be lost instantly, with a single mistake. Thus, a good president secures the trust of his clients, makes deals that are mutually beneficial and objectively settles any disputes or problems that may arise.

MY OWN APPROACH TO MANAGEMENT

We have all heard the story of "The Emperor's New Clothes." While all the emperor's attendants were aware of his folly, and were laughing at him behind his back, they did not hesitate to praise his beautiful garments to his face. All was well until a child cried, "Look! The emperor is naked!" and he awoke to his ignorance. Too many company presidents, I think, are like this emperor. All executives say they don't like "yes men" and then, intentionally or otherwise, surround themselves with people who agree with them. In no time at all the president is out of touch with what's really going on in his firm, but nobody has the guts to tell him. Very often the lowest-ranking members of a firm have a clearer understanding of what's happening to the company than the brass upstairs does. The more an executive cuts himself off from his workers (the people whose efforts really determine the company's success), the more he guarantees that he will be out of touch with the firm's true condition. This is not just bad employee relations; to me it is a sign of incompetent management.

Many companies today, especially larger ones, are run by a board of directors or some similar group. I have no objection to having such a board to act as advisors to the chief executive officer of a firm, as long as they stay out of his way and let him handle the business of running the business. I firmly believe that a ship with one man at the helm is the easiest to steer. I realize the dangers inherent in this, the main one being that it opens the way for a company to be run by a dictator rather than a president. But in the case of my own companies, the president was not elected by popular vote; he was appointed by me or by another president who was appointed by me. Rather than relying on either democratic principles or corporate seniority to choose a leader, we rely on our own instincts. True, it's a kind of gamble. But men who won't gamble on their own good judgment won't succeed for long in this world. Under the system which I have outlined, a strong leader is necessary to breathe life into the new company. If he fails, the company fails. If he succeeds, it is because his own spirit pulled the company through. In this case, I am willing to sacrifice the dubious benefits of rule by committee in favor of a benevolent dictatorship.

The proper attitude

When my first company began to become successful, I was often asked to talk to other managers. But I was afraid of speaking too soon about ideas that I had not fully tested, so I hesitated. Now, after working with *bunsha* for a long time, I've reached the point where I am fully confident of what I have to say. Now I am

invited to give speeches all over the world, and I
don't hesitate to accept. Often my listeners look
surprised by what I say, both here in Japan and
overseas, but I take that as a positive sign. I tell
myself that if people only wanted to hear what
they already knew, they wouldn't ask me to fly
all the way from Tokyo to talk to them, would
they?

Sometimes when I have talked at some
length about how my philosophy affects the
individual rather than the company, a listener
will say, "Mr. Sakai, you seem to place a lot of
value on developing the individual qualities of
your workers."

"Why shouldn't I?" I reply. "Must a corporation be a place where a man's spirit dies
while the company prospers? If so, then it is
nothing but a giant slave ship, with each worker
chained to an oar. Is that what you think a
company should be?"

This always makes people feel a bit foolish, as it is supposed to, but it also brings them
around to saying what they really meant in the
first place: "Mr. Sakai, what you say is all well
and good in theory, but it's... well, it's just a
bit too idealistic. You can't run a corporation
like a kind of big summer camp for your
employees. And let's face it, some employees
need discipline more than coddling."

I like to think that I am an easy-going and
even-tempered man, but this remark almost

always gets me hopping mad, because it means that my listeners have missed the whole point of what I have been saying. And I shouldn't be getting angry at them, for it is ultimately my fault; it means I haven't made myself clear. I generally assume that my audiences are familiar with the realities of business and are also well aware that I have built a highly successful industrial group which has doubled in size in just the past several years. This would not have been possible if we were running a "summer camp" or "coddling" our employees. Nor would it have been possible if we had stuck to old-fashioned ideas of management and employee relations. So let me put this idea to rest right now.

Our companies are not "'summer camps" for anybody, not for employees, not for managers. They are places for work, and every single person who walks through the door in the morning knows that. But knowing that work must be done—and be done efficiently, skillfully and caringly—is not a painful thing, not a depressing or odious thing, in any way. It is merely a fact. What would be truly depressing would be the thought that you must come to work every day, do something that gives you no pleasure, in which you feel no involvement, and from which you derive nothing, only to come back and do it again the next day. To me that is hell on earth, and if that's what it means to run a "realistic" company, I want no part of it.

Another listener once took me by surprise by asking, "What is the most important quality in dealing with life?" Even so, my answer was immediate: "To have a positive attitude and to enjoy life thoroughly is the most important thing for any individual in both his personal and professional life." I firmly believe that the truest sense of happiness begins with a positive attitude toward life. As I said, I have no wish to "coddle" my employees, but I will do everything in my power to see that they have an opportunity to develop that positive attitude towards life. Firstly, this is something we owe each other as human beings, and secondly, it lays the foundation for a strong, positive, well-run and, ultimately, prosperous company. And isn't that what any manager in his right mind wants?

I honestly believe that only by having respect for others and their feelings can we make our businesses truly successful. It is important not only to develop new technologies and produce new products but to make our companies the kind of places in which people enjoy working. This is not just a slogan; I am quite serious about this. Without constantly bearing this idea in mind, it makes no difference if your firm is producing the most sophisticated state-of-the-art technology in any field; to me you're still running a smokestack industry.

Although I am nominally the "head" of dozens of companies, and could easily afford to live like a very well-to-do man, I refuse. Perhaps that is simply my nature, but even if it were not, I would learn to live without the trappings of the affluent executive. For example, it is my feeling that no executive needs a limousine. Nobody. What message are you sending to staff and associates alike by riding in a limousine? That you are rich? Important? Somehow above or different from ordinary people? I would like someone to explain to me how any of these things helps your company.

Of course, it is essential to compensate senior staff for their work, and a good salary and various benefits are absolutely essential for an executive to feel a certain kind of accomplishment. But it can only have a detrimental effect on the company for those who are receiving these considerable salaries to flaunt their wealth in public. Not only is it distasteful, it serves to build an insurmountable wall between them and the other workers. Perhaps this is just what they want, either secretly or not.

When I see executives of some big firms on their way to expensive restaurants in Ginza night after night, I wonder, "When was the last time you had a meal with the people who pay your salary?" I'm sure they would not be able to answer me, because they would have no idea what I was talking about. They don't even realize that those nine-to-five salaried employees in their offices are earning the money that makes it possible for these fellows to live so comfortably on expense accounts. Now, I'm not saying there's anything wrong with going out to a nice restaurant occasionally or using a company expense account to entertain clients; I've done my share of both. But what makes me sick is the number of people I see whose goal is to live this kind of life. More "perks" from the company, more business trips, nicer hotels, better wine, a bigger expense account... you know exactly what I'm talking about. To put it quite simply, I have no use for such men.

In Japan there is an old saying about "eating food from the same pot." It means that those who have lived together, even for a short time, or those who have shared some special experience, are bonded together in a way that is not easily broken. The executive who makes it a point to be seen regularly in the lowest ranks of his company, who eats with the employees, goes drinking with them, goes to parties with them, knows their names and the names of their families—that guy can lead those people to hell and back and not a single one will ever say, "Wait a minute. Am I getting overtime for this?"

I'm sure it won't come as any surprise, then, when I say that I make it a rule to drive my own car. I enjoy driving, and when I have a visitor, I like to take him in my car to see some of the companies in the Taiyo Group. When my visitor is accompanied by a younger assistant, there always seems to be a look of shock on his part that I, an older man and a senior manager at that, will be acting as chauffeur (in Japan, fortunately, there is still some respect shown for both age and position, and a man in my situation is not supposed to perform such menial tasks as driving a car). Thus, I am often implored by some young fellow to let him drive while my guest and I assume the roles of honored fossils in the rear. "Please relax in the backseat," he will eagerly suggest. "I will be happy to drive." I always smile, holding the keys tightly, and as I get in behind the wheel I reply, "Not as happy as I will be. Please relax in back and allow me to enjoy my own car."

In Japan it is also quite common for a younger man to trail around behind a company president, carrying his important papers, attaché case or whatever. While this may denote respect for seniority to some, I think it looks just plain ridiculous. Sometimes when I leave the office for a meeting or am on my way to the airport, some of our younger staff will come rushing up to take my luggage, even when it isn't particularly heavy. "I see," I say to them. "You want to put me in an old-age home as quickly as possible, is that it?" I don't mean to be rude, and they can tell by my smile that I appreciate their good intentions, but I want it clearly understood that simply because I have passed sixty years on this planet does not mean I am an invalid. In recent years science has demonstrated what we all know instinctively, namely, that physical well-being and mental well-being are very closely connected. How can you expect to live a positive life unless you are healthy? I firmly believe that once you start to think you're old, old age is waiting to welcome you.

One thing that keeps me alive and full of energy is talking to people about business. Some men are born to be artists or writers or politicians or maybe cat burglars, but I was born to be a business manager. It's what I do; I do it well and I love it. And I'll be glad to offer advice about good management to anyone who cares to listen, anytime, anywhere. Consequently, upon my retirement from my official duties at Taiyo Industries, I opened a little office in Ginza, both to take care of my own new projects and to receive visitors. I chose Ginza not simply because it is one of the most famous shopping and business districts in Tokyo but because it is in the middle of the city and it is easy for people to find me here. I spend a good deal of time in this office just talking with people.

I suppose I have given many lectures over the years about my management techniques and of course about my view of life (you will have noticed that for me the two are never far apart). At the end of these speeches I tell my listeners that I am always happy to help young managers in need, and that they should feel free to call on me anytime. These days more and more of them are taking me up on the offer. In addition, I seem to have a steady stream of visitors—not only businessmen, but scholars, journalists, government officials and so on. One of my executives joked that I should open a formal consulting office, hang up a shingle outside and put in a waiting room, as I would soon have little time to do any work for the Taiyo Group. This may be a bit of an exaggeration, but the fact is, I don't mind these visits. I find it both pleasant and stimulating to talk with people because I learn something from each one. Furthermore, I am happy to offer what advice I can to men who sincerely want to learn about management. I only wish there had been some experienced manager around to help me with the various problems I was going through during those first several years of Taiyo's growth.

Going public

Not long ago I was visited by a businessman who ran a medium-size machinery company. He said his firm had made rapid progress and he was under considerable pressure from the big securities houses to list his company on the Tokyo Stock Exchange. He was inclined to do so, he said, but wanted to discuss the matter with me first. "The Taiyo Group has shown remarkable growth and yet you haven't listed your companies," he said. "I'm anxious to find out why not. Are you waiting to achieve some certain level of growth?"

I'm afraid my reply was not what he was looking for.

"I will never list my companies for the simple reason that I don't want to sell them into slavery," I said to him. "My firms are not merely legal entities which exist to make profits. They are homes for thousands of people, people who trust me. All of us, from the assembly-line workers to the division managers, company presidents and on up to me, are bound together by a mutual agreement to take care of each other."

Already I was thinking to myself, "Here is another guy about to fall victim to the disease most common among successful small-business executives." Those who contract this disease are usually heads of companies that have recently shown outstanding development. And who transmits this disease? None other than the smiling representatives of highly respected securities companies. I have been called on by many such men from Japan's top brokerage houses, all inviting me to list my companies' stocks and to offer more shares for subscription. Each time I have driven them away, but new brokers, who see only our balance sheets but know nothing of me as a manager, come to beg me to list the Taiyo companies.

In general, they recommend three main advantages of listing: first, considerable funds can be raised for the firm; second, the company becomes much better known; and third, to be blunt, the executives of the firm can make a great deal of money. Some other merits are mentioned, too. For example, by listing stocks, you can recruit talented personnel, give dividends to stockholders and so on. The salesmen tell me that listed stocks circulate wildly in the market and allow the company to raise funds easily from many investors. In short, they are telling me, one can depend for funds on the greed of those who are looking to make easy money by investing.

It is at this point that I ask them who is it that is looking to make easy money? Is it the investors who buy equity in what they believe to be an honest, well-run and profitable enterprise? Or is it the directors of that enterprise who give up control of the company they have built for the sake of overnight riches? This usually causes the salesman to pause for a second in his rapid-fire pitch for my signature. I look at him very sternly and say, "Tell me, would you

sell your children into slavery because somebody made you a good offer?" The look on his
face always says that he doesn't believe I could
be so stupid; he is sure I really do understand
and am just trying to be difficult. But I am not.
I am perfectly serious, foolish as that may
sound to a more "professional" executive. I
care for my firms and I will do everything in my
power to provide for their success until the day
I die. Our employees know that, and I am convinced it makes a difference in everything they
do.

Obviously there are benefits to establishing a joint-stock corporation, especially for a
young and growing company. For one thing, it
enables the management to raise a large amount
of capital quickly and to disperse responsibility
should the company face hard times. As a
result, the executives can relate to their business
with a more relaxed attitude. I agree that for
many reasons this way of setting up a company
makes a great deal of sense on paper. But it
ignores the basic nature of man as a manager,
and thus, in my opinion, it ultimately works
against the best interests of the company. The
management must then decide whether they
wish to act for the long-term good of the company or for their own self-interest? Both are
viable options. No law says that a company
cannot be run essentially to profit its management. I ask only that managers who choose this

course of action have the guts to admit it.

You would think that my pig-headedness about listing our companies' stocks would be the end of it and that the brokers would simply give up on me as a hopeless old fool who doesn't know the value of what he is throwing away. But they persist. If the company borrows money from the bank, they tell me, it must pay it back with interest. If it lists its stock, however, the firm has only to pay a dividend when it shows a profit. If it is managed so as to stay in the red, dividends need never be paid. Besides, they council, even paying dividends is cheaper than paying interest to the bank. So how about it, Mr. Sakai? Please...?

I must truly be a nasty person at heart, because I delight in responding in such a way as to send these fellows into fits. "Actually," I say, "I prefer to borrow money from the bank and return it with high interest."

There is always a short pause at this point while the salesman's eyes bulge and his face changes color.

"What? Are you crazy?"

"I am not. I am old-fashioned, not crazy. I have built my company through honest work and I will manage it through honest means. To me, obtaining easy money for doing nothing is not a proper way to run a company. That is true even if it does not involve selling equity."

But my breath is wasted, for he does not

understand me at all. His eyes say, "Just ask yourself which is easier, to equip your factory with all new equipment through free money, or to do it with money borrowed from the bank? The answer is very simple. Even a child can understand it, so why can't you, Mr. Sakai? Why don't you at least list some of your stocks like a sensible man?" It is evident that he thinks I am an idiot. He even doubts that I have any understanding of a free economy. He probably thinks I am only passing for a corporate executive in a modern capitalistic country when in fact I am a relic from another century. Perhaps he is right.

Alas, it is a fact that the underwriters profit from a listing as well as the executives of the firm they persuade to list, and they are loath to throw in the towel even when confronted with a man as stubborn as myself. And so they do not give up. The next speech goes something like this: the stock price of an unlisted company is not determined. Nobody knows the exact prices of unlisted stocks because they have not been estimated. In the case of unlisted companies, most of the shares are usually held by the owner, although in some companies stocks are held by the employees as well as the owner himself. If a company of the latter type lists its stock, its share price may soar and the employees who have small numbers of shares in their company would suddenly find themselves very well off. And what about the owner? Oh, they say, he would become a billionaire in a single day!

"Just imagine, Mr. Sakai," a salesman from one well-known securities house whispered into my ear. "A billionaire in a single stroke! Think about it!"

"A billionaire?" I shouted. "So what?" Once I have listed the stocks and offered more for subscription, my years of work and my care in managing my companies turn to dust before my eyes. Everything, even the chair I am sitting in and the pen I am writing with, belong to someone else, to thousands of unknown stockholders. I have long since made up my mind. Maybe I could raise capital quickly and easily by listing my stocks. But how would I gain by becoming a giant company overnight? Just being big means nothing to me. It is the "manageable" size of my companies that allows them to maintain what is most important to any business: quality. Not just quality of products and quality of services, but quality of life for each and every person in our companies. What kind of effect would it have on these all-important qualities if our group were to triple in size tomorrow or if Hiroshi and I were to become billionaires overight and decide to go live in Tahiti?

I have made sure that this will not happen to the Taiyo Group. Each company in our group holds shares in the others, not the managers or the individual workers. Although I am called the "owner" of the Taiyo Group, in fact I do not own a single share of stock. If any one of the group companies were to list its stocks, I would not make a single penny, nor would any other individual. To me, selling our stocks publicly would be like selling shares in one's own family to others. Is there any investor in Tokyo or New York or London who would buy our stocks simply out of a deep interest to improve the Taiyo Group companies? Of course not. They would buy the stocks in the hope of making money. They would have full rights as stockholders to share in our profits, but would not bear the responsibility for managing the companies in the first place. The thought of strangers violating my companies in this way makes me ill.

Moreover, how could my employees work under such conditions? Each manager would feel as if he were wearing an ill-fitting suit, and soon even the most stalwart among them would lose interest in their work. People in small companies work for a paycheck like anyone else. But more than that, they work for somebody they know, and this is the kind of "glue" that holds a company together and keeps it functioning properly. People know each other; they are concerned about each other; they respect each other. They may tell jokes about the section chief behind his back, but they'll all go out for a beer together on Friday night. They may complain from time to time about some management decision, but if they're ever really upset, they know immediately who to talk to and they know he'll listen. And anybody who has something important on his mind can walk right into the president's office and speak his piece, because that's the way the system works.

You can't do that very well when the president is responsible to a group of unseen stockholders rather than to his employees. And the feeling he gets of being only "hired help," an expendable functionary answering first to a board of directors, second to a shareholders' meeting, and only occasionally to his own company, weakens his effectiveness as a manager. When even the president feels like only an expensive cog in a big machine, what is the average guy punching a time clock going to think? Yet big companies are almost inevitably run this way, and even smaller companies that decide to list their stocks fall into this trap.

In any case, to finish my discussion of the stockbrokers who even to this day pester me with their offers of rapid corporate growth and overnight riches for me and my friends, let me say that they remind me of the Devil himself whispering in my ear: "Sell yourself, sell your family and be richer than you have ever dreamed of!"

My response is better left unprinted.

On retirement

I believe in selecting capable young leaders to run each new company and encouraging the older leaders to step down as they get on in years. This does not mean that a company should set an arbitrary retirement age. I know some very capable managers who are still active at the age of seventy. However, I chose to retire at fifty, and I hope that the managers of my firms, as they get on into their fifties or early sixties, will begin to think of other ways they can enjoy life and contribute to the group's future success. All our companies value the experience and wisdom of senior managers, and we (for I fall into this category as well) provide a valuable pool of advisors to help current management deal with all kinds of problems. We have not been put out to pasture; we have chosen to retire and devote our energies to other pursuits, but at the same time we are all managers at heart, and we will never give up the desire to keep our hands in business management as long as we are alive. But corporate advisors are most useful when they are just that: advisors. The day-to-day responsibilities of running a company and deciding its policies are best left to younger men.

The key to growth and prosperity is a combination of experience and youthful energy, but neither will come to the fore without the proper environment. Dividing a company provides that environment for two companies, the old and the new. When we select one man and make him the leader of a new company it not only creates new chances for promising workers in the old firm, but also energizes the new leader. If he is an able manager, he may continue to work as long as he wishes (although, as I have said, I would prefer to see him "step up" to the post of advisor). However, he must without fail observe one golden rule: he must divide his company when it reaches a certain level of growth. He cannot cling to it. If he does so, it will grow old, too, and his subordinates will lose their incentive. The duty of every company president is to divide his company when the time comes, giving a younger man a chance to become president of the new firm and dozens, perhaps hundreds, of other employees a chance to start afresh in a new company. This in turn opens up a host of new opportunities in the old firm as well. And if the head of the old firm retires before too long, there will be another shift. This, too, helps to invigorate a company—the knowledge that there is always room for advancement.

This guiding principle is shared by all the leaders of all our companies. I have no doubts whatsoever about the future of the Taiyo Group and the philosophy that has helped it to grow, for I know that long after Hiroshi and I are gone, our successors will transmit the spirit of *bunsha* to those who follow. I am confident of this because I know all our top managers, and they have all learned the truth of this management system directly, through hands-on experience running a company. Every president in the Taiyo Group is expected to lead his men, to build up his company, then to divide it and start building again, to accept all the pains and challenges of leadership without fear. I have actually said to some of our young presidents just starting out, "You must act with courage and intelligence. You must do what you know is right even if others do not support you. You must not fail, for many are depending on you. And if the worst should come, you must meet death bravely." I do not think they misunderstand me.

Policies of the Taiyo Group

Some years ago one of the Taiyo Group firms made OEM computer terminals for a big American company, although at first we could produce only about thirty or forty terminals a month. After a series of trials and failures, we finally discovered a way to turn out high-quality terminals at a rate of about 200 units per month. At that point we gave the technology to the U.S. company.

Most Japanese executives would choke upon reading this and say we were very foolish. They feel a company should not part with a highly sophisticated technology it has developed unless absolutely necessary. I understand their point of view, of course, but this is our policy. Our companies help each other to manufacture the best products possible. However, none of these firms alone is big enough to produce several hundred units a month. Thus, we give other firms the right to manufacture, even if we have developed the techniques ourselves. We were delighted that the American company could produce ten thousand terminals a month using our software, and so in a sense we feel that their success is our success.

Speaking of technical development, I might mention that, in addition to our own research laboratories, we assist with a good deal of experimentation and testing at leading university laboratories or private research institutes across the country. Many of the best scholars and researchers in Japan are working at these R&D think tanks, and our group is pleased to be able to play a part in their work. In effect, our companies provide a vital step between pure research and final mass production. Our engineers help to work out problems in applying new technologies so that research results in techniques that are ready to be put into practice.

I said before that I don't believe one learns

half as much from reading about something as from getting hands-on experience, and this is surely just as true in the applied sciences. Thus, as our people work together with these researchers, they learn about new advances in various fields and find new ways of approaching technical problems. Often a research team will develop a theory for some new technology and ask our engineers to help them to realize it. Before long our own engineers are making suggestions on how to improve the original design. That is the meaning of cooperative research, and it helps us both.

At a discussion with a group of foreign businessmen recently, I was asked a good question pertaining to this point. If our top engineers are forever discussing new research projects with outside people, how can we possibly protect the industrial secrets entrusted to us by our customers? In fact, we always maintain strict confidentiality regarding products and technologies belonging to the companies with whom we have contracts. Some firms in the Taiyo Group have simultaneous OEM contracts for seven or eight rival companies. If even a small secret leaks out, we've lost a customer for good. And once word gets out that we failed to keep just one customer's confidence, we're finished in that business forever. Consequently, we have to work very hard to maintain the strictest secrecy in our plants, and as a result, our customers entrust us with more responsibility every year. I am certain our organization is unique in Japan, and there are probably few like us in the United States. And yet, we have no magic formula, no "secret technique of Japanese management." We simply use the same kind of common sense you would use if you ran a little shop in an old neighborhood instead of a string of modern factories: if people trust you, they'll want to do business with you. If there's even a hint of doubt, they'll take their business elsewhere. Why is it that small companies seem so much better at this than big companies?

What's that Rodin doing in your lobby?

Whenever people visit our offices or factories, they almost always remark about the expressions on the faces of the people they see there. Our managers have grown accustomed to such reactions, and it is not difficult for them to explain how our management system results in people at all levels in a company feeling good about themselves and about their workplace. But what really seems to shock our visitors, and is a bit more difficult to explain, is the selection of exquisite sculpture, painting and other examples of fine art we have on display, even at factories located way out in the countryside. All the items are genuine and some are very expensive, and many a visitor has been forgiven for asking, "What is a beautiful painting like this doing at an electronics factory in the middle of nowhere?"

I display these works for a good reason, and it is related to the reason why our company buildings—all of them—are kept so clean. Would you want to work in a filthy office or in a plant thick with dust and decorated only with a layer of gray paint sprayed over the I-beams and ventilating ducts? Granted, that may be the most economical way to run a factory, but in my experience no one will work to his potential in such an environment. I certainly wouldn't. And what employer in his right mind will knowingly create conditions that allow for less than optimum results from the start? My question is meant to be rhetorical, but I could show you several hundred companies where working conditions are far less than ideal and yet the management is always crying about productivity. To me this is senseless.

If a factory is clean and orderly, it is that much easier for a worker to take a little more pride in his workplace, and thus in his work. Thus, all our offices, plants and facilities are kept clean, not just by management decree, but because the workers themselves want it so. This is only natural. The company is their home for a good part of every day, and they should feel as comfortable as possible being there. This is not a difficult thing to accomplish. I think every manager of every company can achieve better results simply by making his workplace a bit less cold and unfriendly. True, an office needs to look "businesslike," but does that mean it must be sterile and lack human warmth? And if it is not a place where customers need to be received regularly, why shouldn't it be much less "businesslike" (by which we really mean drab and boring) and more "humanlike?" Offices, factories, it makes no difference: these are places where people are going to live and work—hopefully, for years. Let's do everything we can to make them pleasant and comfortable and, if we can, inspirational.

And this is why I choose to spend part of our profits decorating even our most regional factories with works of art. If a workplace is clean and well kept, a person will feel comfortable being there several hours every day. If it is decorated with sculptures by Rodin, or paintings by Picasso, Miró and Chagall, he will feel proud to work there. Furthermore, I believe that an artistic masterpiece is a visible example of an artist's creative efforts, and as such it will always have some influence on its viewers. The energy of these artists may gradually come to have an important influence on the minds of those who see them every day.

Although it may sound strange to some, I can honestly say that as a business manager I was greatly encouraged by works of art. They gave me courage to live when I felt depressed. They showed me that passion and vitality can pass from a man into his work and back again, making both the worker and the work more satisfying. I do not say that companies should spend large sums to acquire originals of famous paintings; that is neither possible nor desirable in many cases. But I can say with firm conviction that the power inherent in art can be of great use in raising workers' morale, and that a manager's ability to appreciate the arts can help to improve the company environment.

ON THE U.S.
AND
JAPAN

I recently had a chance to visit the United States again after a number of years. I have been to the U.S. several times, and I always enjoy these trips. When I first saw America almost thirty years ago, I was a struggling young manager from a relatively poor country, and I was immediately impressed by the overwhelming riches I saw there. Not only the land itself, but the people I met and the tremendous scale of its industry, made a strong impression on me.

My second visit was many years later. Although I was very much aware of how fast Japan was changing, somehow I expected America to be exactly as I remembered it. One day in California I rented a car and went for a drive with a friend, and I was surprised to see how many Japanese cars had appeared on the road. Moreover, there were billboards for famous Japanese companies popping up here and there. I felt a natural sense of pride, both as a Japanese citizen and also because I knew my companies had made some of those products. "So this is where those big firms are marketing our stuff," I thought. Well, good. Foolish as it may sound, I felt almost honored that American consumers thought enough of our products to create a demand for them over there.

But as we drove down the freeway, our rental car suddenly broke down and we had to call for assistance. "You see—you should have rented a Japanese car," my American friend joked, and I thought nothing of it. But as I spent more time in the States and heard the same kind of remarks from dozens of people, not all said in jest, I became more and more concerned. In the interval since my last visit there seemed to have grown a widespread belief among Americans themselves that U.S. industry was failing, and that only the "workaholic" Japanese were capable of producing quality goods in many fields. My colleagues here in Japan will say I should simply have felt great pride that the image of "Made in Japan" could have changed so much in such a short time. Yet in fact it made me feel sad. How could Americans believe their own industry was failing? When an individual loses pride in his work, he will soon lose pride in himself, and I believe this carries over to a nation as well. How could America allow such a thing to happen? I wondered.

At about this time a translation of a book entitled *Japan as Number One* by Harvard professor Ezra Vogel became a best-seller in our country. Many Japanese read this book and swelled with pride because it served to allay the inferiority complex they had developed after our defeat in World War II. Vogel's thesis was that, following its entry into the Vietnam War, the U.S. became weaker and weaker economically, while Japan continued to grow stronger. Needless to say, many Japanese (including a number of responsible business leaders) welcomed this view and concluded that the situation was exactly as described. "America's day is done" began to be heard occasionally when the heads of certain big firms got together, and some went so far as to say that, with the passage of a few years, Japan would soon become the leading nation on earth, although no one seemed to think much about what that would mean. Even today, there are people who hold this view and say that the age of U.S. superiority is over.

But most of us do not believe it, nor do we wish to see it happen. If America ever gives up its mantle of leadership in the free world, who will benefit? Who would take up the torch if America's hand were to falter? Not Japan, that is certain. Therefore, like many Japanese executives, I have been happy to see the U.S. experiencing a resurgence of pride in American business and industry.

This may sound strange to many Americans (who, my friends there tell me, see us Japanese as "economic animals" trying to gobble up the world), but it is a simple fact that the average Japanese looks up to the United States in a way that he does to no other country. And this is not only true of the older generation who remember the occupation; almost every university student in Japan hopes to make a trip to the U.S. upon his or her graduation, much as Americans once went to Europe in an earlier era. American fashion, film, food, music and yes, even manufactured goods are visible everywhere in Japan today and their influence is growing. And those of us in the business world are well aware that without the support of the American economy our current affluence would not exist. Today more than ever our two economies are intertwined, and our destinies linked more strongly than either side is willing to admit. True, in many industrial fields we are rivals, but is that such a bad thing? Hasn't our competition forced us both to make better and better products, and haven't people worldwide benefited as a result? I pray that we will come to realize that our mutual interests as partners far outweigh our problems as competitors.

This is not to belittle our political and trade problems, nor to pretend that new ones will not arise—that is inevitable even when two people try to live together in harmony, much less two nations. Rather, I mean to say that we must look to the future of our two countries and the world, and so find ways to solve our problems rather than fight about them.

And as for America, I have seen with my own eyes that she is as full of drive and as dynamic as always. Too many Japanese tend to go to extremes in looking at our most important neighbor: they either wildly extol the U.S. as the symbol of Western culture or dismiss it in a breath as "over the hill." They are not aware of the surprising latent power of its people, like a muscle that lies unseen until it is flexed. We have not caught up with America at all. Perhaps it has yielded the manufacture of certain goods to Japan, for efficient production is what we excel in. Yet America has no equal in the most important fields, such as aircraft design, space exploration, computer science, finance and biochemistry. America is still a world leader and will be throughout my children's and grandchildren's lifetimes.

As my visits to the U.S. have grown more frequent in the past few years, this feeling has grown more certain. Consequently, I have expanded our group's business with American firms and will continue to do so. I am proud to have been invited by a number of American universities and various business organizations to speak to them about *bunsha*. This is most rewarding to me personally, for if my philosophy of "smaller is better" management and concern for one's employees can take root in the fertile soil of American enterprise, I am certain it will grow and flourish. From what I have read about American business in the past few years, this trend is already visible to some extent among managers of small and medium-size businesses, but its principles and goals have not yet been clearly articulated. I hope that what I say here will be well received and put into practice in the United States and Canada.

THE REAL SECRETS
OF JAPANESE
MANAGEMENT

Whenever I speak overseas about my management philosophy, many businessmen ask me, "Is this normal Japanese management practice?" "Absolutely not," I reply. "It's my own method, and I use it for a simple reason: it works." In the past decade the so-called "Japanese way of management" has drawn a lot of attention from foreign companies. Such traditions as lifetime employment, a seniority system, quality control circles and personalized employee relations have been recommended by Western business analysts as the "secret weapons" of running a successful company. Why did these things suddenly receive so much attention? Perhaps because our economy has grown so dramatically in the past few decades, and it seemed to many as if there must be some secret key to the "Japanese miracle."

If I were a manager of a Western company, I would not put much trust in this obsession with the "Japanese way of management." I do not say that it is worthless, only that what is perceived as the Japanese system is neither widespread nor of very long standing here in Japan. Some of the aspects that Western writers have singled out are interesting, often useful and quite possibly "exportable" to other societies. What they fail to see are the deeper values which underlie these superficial systems and the fact that we will be quick to change the system when circumstances dictate. Economic pressures are now bringing about rapid changes in certain parts of Japanese business (the finance sector comes readily to mind) and will undoubtedly spread to other businesses as well. Already some of our leading corporations have begun to study "the Western way of management" in search of solutions to these problems.

What I do find interesting about all this, however, is that not long ago economists worldwide were criticizing Japan for our seniority system, lifetime employment, family allowance and so on. These were, they said, critical weaknesses of Japanese management. They warned us that unless we corrected these defects, Japan would never be strong economically. Then, in just a few years, they turned around 180 degrees and began to applaud these "weak" systems. While I would not want to cast doubts on the credibility of professional economists, I cannot help but marvel at the flexibility of their theories.

When I said that the so-called Japanese system of lifetime employment, etc., is not widespread, I also meant to point out a very basic but often overlooked fact about Japanese business. When economists talk about Japanese theories of management, they are usually looking only at major industry. Yet, in fact, more than 90% of Japanese industry is minor industry. Relatively few companies have more than three hundred employees, and more than three-quarters of all Japanese companies are very small, employing only a handful of people. The real backbone of the Japanese economy is not the Toyotas and Nissans, the Matsushitas and Sonys, the Fujitsus and NECs, but rather, the thousands upon thousands of small firms that allow these behemoths to exist in the first place. It is a simple fact that Japan's internationally famous companies would not exist without the support of a myriad unknown small businesses nationwide. Thus, whether Japan will remain strong or not depends to a large extent on its small and medium-size companies. Too many people, economists and business analysts alike, seem to be attracted by the glamor of the giant firms and miss the real heart of Japanese business. Thus, when I read a few years ago of Western executives studying what was being sold to them as the "Japanese art of management," I knew that they were way off course, looking at the activities of only a tiny, though highly visible, fragment of Japanese business.

While we're on the subject, I might mention that when I was last in the U.S. I chanced to look at a magazine article on the subject of Japanese management (how could I resist?). I was astonished to learn from this piece that "the time-honored traditions of Japanese management helped the country to survive the oil crises of the '70s..." and so on. I'm sorry to say I could not help laughing then and there, for this is total nonsense.

Japan has overcome both externally imposed and domestic crises, thanks to the fundamental values in our culture, not to the management traditions of big companies. For example, we have always believed in frugality. Even today, when our society has reached heights of affluence unimaginable just a generation ago, and people are spending more to acquire more goods, we still have the highest personal savings rate of any industrialized country (something we are now being scolded for, as it is detrimental to the balance of world trade). The concept of "smaller is better" was not the brainstorm of an overworked research engineer at Sony; its roots go far back in Japanese tradition, and examples of this way of thinking abound in Japanese life. Someone once suggested to me that Japanese cars were well designed to weather the two big oil shocks. An interesting comment, I admit, but the young man seemed not to have noticed that Japan had been making small cars for decades before there was an oil crisis. We have not made big, wasteful automobiles not because we were forced to economize, but simply because we have never thought of making large, wasteful cars. Imagine that a promising oil field were suddenly to be discovered in Japan and overnight we became one of the world's biggest oil-producing countries. Would our automakers suddenly start producing gas-guzzling land yachts? Of course not, because as a culture we still cling to that "smaller is better" mentality, even when we can afford to trade it in on a bigger model.

As you know, I, too, am an ardent supporter of "smaller is better" thinking and a harsh critic of allowing things to grow too big for their own good. As I said at the beginning of this book, Japan taught the world the virtue of this philosophy in the field of consumer goods, but completely missed the boat when it came to applying the same logic to its corporations. Thus, we have allowed our best companies to grow into giant conglomerates, losing much of the talent and energy that made them great along the way. With every passing day they become more like "stuffed tigers" and less like the creative, dynamic institutions they pretend to be. How, then, do they continue to survive and prosper? The answer is simple, but it requires an understanding of something that seems to have drawn little attention so far in the West: the Japanese subcontractor system.

The Japanese subcontractor system

Several American friends who read a draft of this book said they were surprised to see how long I remained loyal to the firm I called Miyamoto Electronics and how unwilling I was to sever relations with them at a much earlier stage. "If they treated you so badly, why didn't you break away sooner and make a go of it on your own?" was a typical comment. I must say, these remarks made me smile, for it is just this spirit of independence that I find so admirable in American business. However, it also shows a total lack of understanding of the Japanese system, and I suppose this is what really surprised me.

Whenever I travel abroad these days I make it a point to peruse local bookstores, and, as I noted before, I am always amused to see dozens of books called *Understanding Japanese Management Strategy* or *The Real World of Japanese Business*, or some such thing. I have seen books illustrating how to exchange business cards and where to sit in a taxi when riding with Japanese guests—even books filled with important vocabulary for Western businessmen to use when negotiating with us cagey Japanese. With all this information available, I assumed that most foreign businessmen were by now well acquainted with the *shitauke* (subcontractor) system that has been the basis of Japanese business and industry for generations. Yet, after talking with some foreign business friends in Tokyo and associates in the U.S. and Europe, I discovered that even today little is known or published about this rather important aspect of our society. Perhaps Western writers don't really understand it, or perhaps the big companies to whom they go in researching their books don't want them to understand it. *Shitauke* is definitely not a word one brings up in trying to establish good relations with a large Japanese company with whom you are trying to sign a contract. In any case, I think the time has come to bring the subject to light.

The *shitauke* (pronounced "sh'ta-ookay") system is in one sense the very foundation of our modern business and industrial structure, the base upon which our giant commercial structure has been built. In this sense, it is important merely in helping to understand the structure of the Japanese economy, especially in the post-war period. More specifically, it is one of the keys to understanding the famous "Japanese miracle" of the past few decades. And lastly, but perhaps most importantly, it is essential information for any foreign business trying to tie up with or contract business from a large Japanese firm. If one understands how large corporations in a wide variety of fields act merely as "trading companies," farming out jobs to their affiliates at cut-rate prices while charging their clients for the prestige of dealing with a top-notch Japanese firm, one has a great deal more leverage to use in negotiating. And the firm that is able to by-pass the big "name" companies and go directly to their subcontractors, affiliates or subsidiaries will discover that the Japanese quality they are looking for need not have a high price tag.

There are four basic types of Japanese sub-contractors. The first is simply invested in by a holding company. The second is managed by a director transferred from the parent company. The third employs retired personnel from the parent company. The fourth has no formal connection with the major contractor except to fulfill orders. Obviously, the first three are closer to the top of the pyramid—that is, closer to the parent firm, and thus will be looked after to a greater extent by the parent. The fourth type is the base of the pyramid, the most common and also of the least concern to the parent firm. Most of these firms are small, but a few, like my own, grow to a respectable size, and become major producers for a big corporate group. But regardless of where they are in this hierarchy, all the many subcontractors owe total allegiance to the parent firm.

I am sure there are subcontractors in the United States and Europe which are also heavily influeced by their major customers, and yet I suspect that the system in our country is rather different. In Japan, most small firms (and nearly all small manufacturing firms) exist in the shadow of a few dozen giant corporations which completely control their destinies. In the West you know the names of many of these giant corporations, especially in the consumer electronics and automobile fields, for instance. But underneath each big "name" company are hundreds upon hundreds of smaller companies whose survival depends on supplying parts or semi-finished units to the larger firms. They are rarely under contract to more than two, and in most cases the small companies are nothing more than slaves to a single industrial giant. For a small subcontractor to trade with a large firm on an equal footing may be regarded as a matter of course in Western nations, but it is impossible to imagine in Japan. Traditionally, if a subcontractor were to accept an order from a client other than his "master" company, he would almost surely have to face some very serious consequences (as I mentioned in discussing my own company's history). The master firm completely controls both its subcontractors' production levels and unit costs, and this is the reason the giant industrial combines so jealously guard this system.

Let us consider a simple example in a field that I know well. Imagine a fictitious electronics maker, whom we will call Tobishi Hitatsu K.K. Tobishi Hitatsu is a huge firm involved in all kinds of electric and electronic products, from consumer appliances to computers to industrial power generators. Of course, Tobishi has a dozen or so large factories scattered throughout Japan, and beautiful aerial photos of these ultramodern facilities adorn their office walls and annual reports. But even a child can see that these few factories are not enough to produce all the products the firm manufactures. Obviously they must purchase a large portion of their goods on an OEM basis, that is, as either finished or semi-finished products manufactured by another company.

What many people, even here in Japan, would find surprising is the astounding quantity of goods the firm purchases rather than manufactures. These goods easily make up a very large percentage of its entire product line. Where does it obtain these goods? From its factories, or so it says. In fact, many of the products may even pass through one of Tobishi's factories at some point, but most are completely finished and assembled before they ever reach Tobishi, waiting only for the firm to put its name on the outer case and send the products out through its international distribution and marketing system. For under the control of each one of its factories is a network of perhaps two dozen or so prime subcontractors, firms that probably do not bear the Tobishi name but are very closely tied to its industrial "group." These may be, for example, final assembly lines that merely put together a few basic components comprising scores or even hundreds of smaller parts which were pre-assembled by another company.

Underneath these few dozen prime subcontractors is another level of hundreds of secondary subcontractors. These firms are also part of the Tobishi Hitatsu Group in that they receive all their orders from a main subcontractor to a Tobishi factory. And under this level of subcontractors lies a third, even larger group and, in most cases, a fourth made up of several hundred very small shops, perhaps producing only one specialty part in each. If we were to count all the firms of any size that are part of this one industrial pyramid, there would easily be 500, and in many cases more like 1,000–1,500 individual companies working for Tobishi Hitatsu. But only a very few are rewarded with the Tobishi Group name, only those few get their photos on the wall of the head office and only those few are part of the system of "lifetime employment" that is so often talked about in Western descriptions of Japanese management.

Of course, it would seem logical for this vast network of subcontractors to pull together, working for the good of the "parent" conglomerate, which would in turn take care of them. And, to a limited degree, this does happen. The various upper levels of the hierarchy usually pass down enough orders to keep those below from going out of business. This is ot merely benevolence on the part of the Tobishi factories; it is seential to keep a number of small subcontractors producing the same parts so that they can compete with each other, thus increasing production efficiency and paring down their costs. Competition among subcontractors is good for the parent, and as you may remember from my own experiences trying to make Taiyo Industries into a principle supplier for our parent company, sometimes it is deemed appropriate to divide up the orders even when one subcontractor is far ahead of the rest in both price and quality. This serves two functions: it keeps the other small firms from failing, and also leaves them that much more indebted to the parent that has "rescued" them by tossing some orders their way.

If I seem to be painting these giant corporations as exploitative, ruthless and mercenary, please forgive me. That is exactly what my experience of over forty years has shown them to be—at least, when it comes to dealing with the various levels of companies who depend upon them for their existence.

I said before that the subcontractor system is one of the key factors in the stupendous growth that is sometimes referred to as the "Japanese economic miracle." Let's look at that a bit closer. One way to explain the primary function of this hierarchical subcontractor system is to imagine it as an "industrial shock absorber." We don't have to go all the way back to the 1960's or even the oil shocks of the 1970's for a good example. Let's imagine that it's early in 1986 and the value of the yen is suddenly beginning to soar against the U.S. dollar. Tobishi Hitatsu Corp. depends heavily on exports for its income. If the yen rises with respect to foreign currencies, the prices of its goods in overseas markets will have to rise accordingly, which will cut sharply into its high market shares. When its products are no longer so competitively priced, demand will fall and the firm's exports will dwindle. The result? Tobishi (and other large manufacturers) will be badly squeezed, and Japan's trade surplus with foreign nations will drop within a few months. Or so it was predicted by many leading foreign economists.

The problem with this scenario was that it assumed that Tobishi and firms like it had their backs to the wall. Even if the company instituted severe austerity measures in all its offices (one industry giant, we read that year, was saving little scraps of paper to eliminate the need to buy note pads), there was really little room for belt-tightening, and so the firm would have to raise export prices almost immediately to offset its loss in revenue. This shows a complete lack of understanding of Japanese industry, for belt-tightening is precisely the function of the *shitauke* system. This giant invisible "shock absorber" was one main reason why export prices of Japanese goods climbed only marginally in that year while the yen doubled in value against the dollar.

Whereas costs in most industries are more or less fixed and only their profit margins can be cut, most large Japanese corporations can actually control their costs. Thus, as the yen began to skyrocket, Tobishi sent word to its primary subcontractors that as of the following month all orders would be cut by 30% in volume and the unit price charged by the subcontractor to Tobishi would be cut by 40%. Fortunately for the primary subcontractor, he has his own cushion to fall back on. He tells the various smaller firms who supply him with goods that as of next week all orders will be cut by 40% and prices by 50%. This goes on and on down the line, leaving, as you can imagine, the hundreds of tiny shops at the bottom of the organization with an impossible situation. Merely to stay alive, they must lay off workers immediately, defer salaries for those that remain, borrow money from any source they can find and so on. In many cases they simply go out of business and one of their rivals somehow manages to fill enough of both orders to stay afloat. The important fact to remember is that these subcontractors have no choice. They are owned, body and soul, by the industrial group to which they belong. Even if one had thoughts about trying to break free and doing business with another domestic firm, he would find himself out in the cold: no one wants a deserter in their outfit, even if he comes cheap.

The advantages for the parent firm are just as obvious as the disadvantages for the smaller firms. If the giant corporation falls on hard times, it does not need to lay off employees or radically alter any part of its own corporate structure. If battens down the hatches and rides out the storm for a couple of years (and issues press bulletins about how its secretaries are saving scraps of paper), but its inconvenience is kept to a minimum. When conditions improve, it unfurls the sails and returns to business as usual. Of course, as a result of its policies a host of smaller firms may sink, but that is of little consequence. There are always more small firms eager to take their places. Meanwhile, it holds on to a large chunk of its market share overseas, and, with production costs squeezed to the bone, actually increases the profit margin on its domestic sales, where retail prices were higher in the first place! Investors at home and abroad note with approval that the firm has survived adverse business conditions that should by all rights have cut deeply into profits for the past few years, and Tobishi's stock price rises accordingly. The firm's operations are now leaner, more profitable and better prepared to take on whatever changes the markets will require in the future. All thanks in large part to those several hundred invisible firms absorbing the impact that would normally have crippled the parent company.

Is this a good situation for the Japanese economy? Unquestionably. Is it a good situation for business and industry as a whole? That is a very difficult question for me to answer. Clearly, the flexibility of this system has allowed our economy to withstand a number of shocks and recover quickly. It has helped individual companies to survive tough times until market conditions improved. Viewed from this perspective, the subcontractor system is a boon to industry and an important asset of the economy as a whole, and we should work to preserve it. But from my own experience, having served as one of these "slave" companies for many years, I see another side of the issue.

I believe very strongly that a situation in which one company must produce at another's beck and call is ultimately destructive. Who, either manager or employee, can be motivated to perform his best in such a situation? You feel like a slave, toiling away day and night to help feed an unseen giant who neither knows nor cares for your existence. In this case, however, many would argue that the giant is fighting daily to protect our country, and his health and welfare are all of our concern. In addition, the giant himself helps to feed thousands of others whom we do not see. Is not our sacrifice, and that of hundreds of other companies like our own, justified by his need to compete with foreign rivals?

I do not think so, and for two good reasons: these small companies are not slaving away to help some lean, hungry business stay in peak form, or to ward off challenges from abroad. In fact, most of the corporate giants they work for are fat, lazy, inefficient, often badly managed and lacking in the creative energy that made them industrial leaders in the first place. Moreover, they are not fighting to uphold Japan's standard against foreign competitors half as much as they are struggling to win a small percentage of market share from their domestic rivals. So the argument that "What is good for Dai Nippon Widget K.K. is good for Japan" doesn't carry a lot of weight with me. These companies were all once trim, hungry, efficient and competitive. Now they are "competitive" only to the extent that the products they obtain from their subcontractors are better than the products their rivals obtain from their subcontractors. Are these the kind of corporate standard-bearers we Japanese should be proud of? I don't think so.

I do think we should begin to recognize these companies for what they are. And I think businesses worldwide should begin to overcome their awe and admiration of these famous Japanese conglomerates. Yes, they do perform valuable research, they do develop and apply some important technologies and, yes, they do even produce a variety of products on their own (although almost always large-volume products with high profit margins). But the simple, irrefutable fact is that the real power of our industry lies in smaller, highly advanced companies who sell OEM products to these giants or do their assembly, their design, their construction or whatever for them. Of course the big firms don't want foreign companies to know where they buy their products or how cheaply these goods really are, and they certainly don't want you to find out that you could buy exactly the same products for which you have contracted to a big Japanese company famed for its "brilliant research" by going directly to the source of that research—the little companies who developed the products in the first place.

I suppose that, being so heavily involved in manufacturing myself, I tend to focus too much on this one area when it comes to the role of the subcontractor, and so I have used an example from that industry I am closest to. Yet, this phenomenon exists not only in manufacturing but in construction, advertising, publishing and a dozen other fields as well. We Japanese are fairly accustomed to this practice, and we assume that one of the functions of a large company is to locate, oversee and guarantee the work of the smaller firms that do most of its work. The fact that we pay twice for the same job is just built into the system. No one complains and no one seems eager to change things.

But now, with foreign companies clamoring for ways to compete in the Japanese market and do away with "non-tariff barriers," it seems the time is ripe for someone to say, "Why should we pay All-Nippon Heavy Industries to handle that job when they're just going to turn around and give it to somebody else? If we can get exactly the same thing from the original maker at a lower cost, what are we waiting for?"

Of course, should a Western firm even hint to one of these giant firms that it knows there are other players in the game, the company's representatives will laugh and say, "Of course we have subcontractors. Don't you, too? But they're really quite small and certainly not capable of supplying the kind of work you're looking for." Then, very sternly, in case you didn't get the message about what it is you're paying for, they will say, "And besides, we couldn't possibly guarantee the quality of anything they might produce." If you insist on being difficult about this subcontractor issue, they will guarantee that whatever it is you want, whether it be manufacturing an optical disk reader, constructing a new building or designing a new advertising program, the work will be handled exclusively by their own staff, an in-house project from start to finish. They will keep this up until you are convinced at last, mop your brow at the thought of the mistake you almost made and reach for your pen. The next day the division manager in charge of the project will get on the phone and decide which firm to give it to.

The other day I was having lunch in a Tokyo restaurant with the president of one of the electronics firms in our group. We discussed business in general and he filled me in on some new technological developments the firm had made, including the ability to produce a new kind of computer-related equipment. I was impressed. What were the prospects for selling the device? Oh, he replied, the firm would soon start production of several thousand units a month for the local arm of a giant American computer company. Really? Now I was even more impressed. How did we land the contract with the U.S. firm? "We didn't," he replied, busy with his soup. "We were one of eight bidders, and our bid was very good, but the U.S. company decided to give it to one of the bigger, more well-established firms. Now they're trying to decide whether to go with M—— or S——."

"Well, then," I said. "What makes you say we're going to start up production?"

"Simple," he said, pausing for a moment to smile. "Both M—— and S—— have already approached us to make the unit for them in case they get the contract."

It's nice to hear good news from my managers, but I'm afraid this story is not so unusual

these days, and I'm beginning to wonder how
much longer it will go on. How much longer
will foreign firms continue to do business in
this way? If I were a stockholder of such a firm,
I would be up in arms at the idea of the company squandering money like this and then
complaining about how expensive it is to do
business with the Japanese. The Taiyo Group is
certainly not the only one of its kind in Japan.
There must be thousands of high-quality companies out there, subcontracting for bigger firms
with prestigious names. I suspect a growing
number of these companies would welcome a
chance to take on work by themselves and
prove that just because their names are not
household words does not mean that they cannot do a first-rate job for a very competitive
price. And this means in every industry, in
every major field of business in Japan. If just a
few firms made a success of it, more would
have the courage to try. Ultimately I don't
believe that this will hurt the giant corporations
very much; it will only force them to get back
to basics and stop functioning as trading
companies.

The very fact that I have mentioned this in
print may raise a good deal of criticism in my
own country. Several big firms may publish
articles to show that they are really still centers
of research and pillars of the Japanese economy.
They may deny everything I have said, or they

may just ignore it and hope I go away. Over the years, the big electronics firms have grown accustomed to my constant criticism of their ways, but since my companies turn out good products which make them look good, they have generally tried to ignore me. In any case, I think they are hoping that the Almighty will summon me soon to do some management reorganization elsewhere.

But many others will misunderstand what I am saying. People will accuse me of being "unpatriotic," and say that I do not have Japan's best interests at heart or that I am "selling out" to foreign businesses. They may call me disloyal or say I am trying to eviscerate Japanese industry, when in fact nothing could be further from the truth. I have been trying for decades to develop ideas to strengthen industry, to show companies how to become more efficient, more profitable and more humane in the process. I honestly believe that the ideas I have called *bunsha* are the only sure way to provide for the future success of business and industry in the coming century, and that clinging to the ideas of the past will only hasten the demise of our prominence.

Thus I feel it is time for our larger companies to truly "rationalize." Not by growing bigger and more centralized, but by breaking up, decentralizing and revitalizing their business. In short, by rediscovering what it means to be competitive, by giving their component parts a chance to rediscover their own potential for productivity and creativity, and letting these new "groups" of smaller companies prove that they are even stronger than the sum of their parts, stronger than any large company with semi-autonomous "divisions" and a central bureaucracy could ever be.

A BETTER WAY

Whenever I give a speech I usually close by talking about "a better way." This should come as no surprise to you, my readers, who have seen what it is I am striving for. As I mentioned earlier, I have been refining my ideas about business management for over forty years. I believe that keeping a company young, vital and full of drive is the essence of good management, yet I see companies everywhere growing old and inflexible. They forget that it is man, not money, that is the driving force of business. And man achieves full satisfaction in any enterprise only when he knows that he is a vital component of that venture. As a company grows larger, the number of people who feel directly responsible for its success grows ever smaller. As more employees feel uninvolved with the company's existence, they have little interest in their own work. The result is predictable: even in good companies we find a small core of energetic and committed managers who feel that to succeed they must somehow drag the dead weight of the rank-and-file workers forward. What idiocy!

Company division (and the management philosophy that goes with it) allows all employees, top to bottom, to feel that they play an integral part in the firm's success. If properly employed, it will energize an entire work force and produce startling results. The key, once again, is to make individuals and their needs a primary concern of management. In each of our companies there are signs that might be roughly translated as "Work hard and enjoy yourself"—and we mean it. If a person does not gain any satisfaction from his or her life, what is the point of it? If satisfaction is achieved only outside the work place, the company is suffering. I absolutely believe that all employees in all enterprises ought to work hard as a logical result of their contentment within their working environment. If not, only management is to blame. The optimum situation is one in which each worker performs his job with pleasure and is reasonably compensated for his labor. I do not see how this goal can be achieved except by dividing a company.

In Japan there is a simple word, *nuruma-yu*, which means "lukewarm water." It is often used to refer to a common situation in all our lives and a too-common situation in business. When our bathwater is lukewarm, we aren't really happy, because we'd like it to be hotter, but at the same time it's not all that cold, so we aren't about to give up and get out. As long as the water stays lukewarm, we are content to remain in a state of mediocrity—not achieving what we know is possible, but satisfied that things aren't as bad as they could be. When I talk to managers at big companies today, this is exactly the impression I get. Sure, things could be better in the best of all possible worlds, but they could also be a lot worse. That's *nuruma-yu* thinking, and it's strangling us.

Which is why I say to managers of companies everywhere, large and small: Give up the ideas of over-reaching for growth. Wake up to the potential that lies dormant within your office, your factory, your corporate system. Real, lasting, meaningful success for every part of your company is right under your nose! You don't need expensive seminars or rousing company songs or a change in personnel. What you do need is guts, common sense and vision. Stop tolerating mediocrity!

There is a better way.

Afterword

Although I have not discussed his contributions in these pages, the late Prof. Takasuke Nakayama was a scholar, businessman and poet whom I loved and respected deeply. It was thanks to his teachings that I was able to overcome many of the difficulties I faced in the early years of my first company. After his death I established a memorial hall to preserve his teachings and honor his memory.

Years ago he told me that he wanted to "live with the spirit of a dandelion."

"Why?" I said. "I'm not sure I understand."

"A dandelion," he replied, "has its spores distributed far and wide by the wind. The fallen spores will take root almost anywhere, put forth buds and bloom in the spring, like a person who accepts his place under heaven, never complains and lives with all the energy at his command. New spores are then carried to faraway places, take root and flower in succeeding springs. The dandelion's life is short, but its spirit lives on and on. Is this not a wonder of Nature?"

And now, at last I can say that I understand his feelings, because I have a dream to see my ideas about company management spread far and wide, even long after I am gone. I want to teach people that company division is both rewarding and practical, regardless of where a company is located or what it does, and that controlled growth can keep any business young, vital and healthy. I am confident that this idea will take root in many different soils and will grow and take on a life of its own even when I am long since departed. But while I live I will continue to lecture and write in order to spread this idea which I call *bunsha*.